D0385585

THE YALE SHAKESPEARE

EDITED BY

WILBUR L. CROSS   TUCKER BROOKE

WILLARD HIGLEY DURHAM

PUBLISHED UNDER THE DIRECTION

OF THE

DEPARTMENT OF ENGLISH, YALE UNIVEPSITY.

ON THE FUND

GIVEN TO THE YALE UNIVERSITY PRESS IN 1917

BY THE MEMBERS OF THE

KINGSLEY TRUST ASSOCIATION

TO COMMEMORATE THE SEVENTY-FIFTH ANNIVERSARY

OF THE FOUNDING OF THE SOCIETY

·: The Yale Shakespeare :·

THE SECOND PART OF
KING HENRY THE FOURTH

EDITED BY

SAMUEL B. HEMINGWAY

NEW HAVEN · YALE UNIVERSITY PRESS
LONDON · GEOFFREY CUMBERLEGE
OXFORD UNIVERSITY PRESS

TABLE OF CONTENTS

The facsimile opposite represents the title-page of the Elizabethan Club copy of the only early Quarto Edition.

THE
Second part of Henrie

the fourth, continuing to his death,
and coronation of Henrie
the fift.

With the humours of sir Iohn Fal-
staffe, and swaggering
Pistoll.

As it hath been sundrie times publikely
acted by the right honourable, the Lord
Chamberlaine his seruants.

Written by William Shakespeare.

LONDON
Printed by V.S. for Andrew Wise, and
William Aspley.
1600.

[DRAMATIS PERSONÆ.]

RUMOUR, *the Presenter*

KING HENRY THE FOURTH

PRINCE HENRY, *afterwards crowned King Henry the Fifth*

PRINCE JOHN OF LANCASTER, ⎫ *Sons to Henry the Fourth,*
HUMPHREY OF GLOUCESTER, ⎬ *and brethren to Henry the*
THOMAS OF CLARENCE, ⎭ *Fifth*

NORTHUMBERLAND, ⎫
THE ARCHBISHOP OF YORK, ⎪
MOWBRAY, ⎪
HASTINGS, ⎬ *Opposites against King Henry*
LORD BARDOLPH, ⎨ *the Fourth*
TRAVERS, ⎪
MORTON, ⎪
COLEVILE, ⎭

WARWICK, ⎫
WESTMORELAND, ⎪
SURREY, ⎪
GOWER, ⎬ *Of the King's Party*
HARCOURT, ⎨
[BLUNT], ⎪
LORD CHIEF JUSTICE, ⎭

[*Servant to the Lord Chief Justice*]

POINS, FALSTAFF, BARDOLPH, PISTOL, PETO, PAGE, *Irregular Humorists*

SHALLOW and SILENCE, *Both Country Justices*

DAVY, *servant to Shallow*

FANG and SNARE, *two sergeants*

MOULDY, SHADOW, WART, FEEBLE, BULLCALF, *Country Soldiers*

[*Porter at Warkworth Castle*]

[FRANCIS, *a Drawer*]

Drawers, Beadles, Grooms

[Lords and Attendants, Officers and Soldiers]

NORTHUMBERLAND'S WIFE

PERCY'S WIDOW

HOSTESS QUICKLY

DOLL TEARSHEET

EPILOGUE

Dramatis Personæ; *cf. App. C*   Opposites: *adversaries*
Irregular: *lawless, unconventional*   Drawer: *waiter*

The Second Part of
King Henry the Fourth

INDUCTION

[Warkworth. Before Northumberland's Castle]

Enter Rumour, painted full of tongues.

Rum. Open your ears; for which of you will stop
The vent of hearing when loud Rumour speaks?
I, from the orient to the drooping west,
Making the wind my post-horse, still unfold   4
The acts commenced on this ball of earth:
Upon my tongues continual slanders ride,
The which in every language I pronounce,
Stuffing the ears of men with false reports.   8
I speak of peace, while covert enmity
Under the smile of safety wounds the world:
And who but Rumour, who but only I,
Make fearful musters and prepar'd defence,   12
Whilst the big year, swoln with some other grief,
Is thought with child by the stern tyrant war,
And no such matter? Rumour is a pipe
Blown by surmises, jealousies, conjectures,   16
And of so easy and so plain a stop
That the blunt monster with uncounted heads,
The still-discordant wavering multitude,
Can play upon it. But what need I thus   20
My well-known body to anatomize
Among my household? Why is Rumour here?

S. d. Enter Rumour, etc.; *cf. n.*   2 vent: *aperture*   4 still: *always*
17 stop: *hole in wind instrument by which difference of pitch is obtained*

I run before King Harry's victory;
Who in a bloody field by Shrewsbury   24
Hath beaten down young Hotspur and his troops,
Quenching the flame of bold rebellion
Even with the rebels' blood. But what mean I
To speak so true at first? my office is   28
To noise abroad that Harry Monmouth fell
Under the wrath of noble Hotspur's sword,
And that the king before the Douglas' rage
Stoop'd his anointed head as low as death.   32
This have I rumour'd through the peasant towns
Between the royal field of Shrewsbury
And this worm-eaten hole of ragged stone,
Where Hotspur's father, old Northumberland,   36
Lies crafty-sick. The posts come tiring on,
And not a man of them brings other news
Than they have learn'd of me: from Rumour's tongues
They bring smooth comforts false, worse than true
    wrongs.   *Exit.* 40

ACT FIRST

Scene One

[*The Same*]

Enter Lord Bardolph, at one door.

L. Bard. Who keeps the gate here? ho!

    [*Enter the Porter above.*]

                        Where is the earl?

Port. What shall I say you are?

24 Shrewsbury; *cf. n.*
33 peasant: *provincial*
37 crafty-sick: *feigning sickness*
2 What: *who*

29 Harry Monmouth; *cf. n.*
35 hole; *cf. n.*
tiring: *riding until they are tired*

L. Bard.   **Tell thou the earl**
That the Lord Bardolph doth attend him here.
   Port. His Lordship is walk'd forth into the
      orchard: 4
Please it your honour knock but at the gate,
And he himself will answer.

Enter Northumberland.

   L. Bard.   Here comes the earl.
   North. What news, Lord Bardolph? every minute
      now
Should be the father of some stratagem.   8
The times are wild; contention, like a horse
Full of high feeding, madly hath broke loose
And bears down all before him.
   L. Bard.   Noble earl,
I bring you certain news from Shrewsbury.   12
   North. Good, an God will!
   L. Bard.   As good as heart can wish.
The king is almost wounded to the death;
And, in the fortune of my lord your son,
Prince Harry slain outright; and both the Blunts   16
Kill'd by the hand of Douglas; young Prince John
And Westmoreland and Stafford fled the field;
And Harry Monmouth's brawn, the hulk Sir John,
Is prisoner to your son: O! such a day,   20
So fought, so follow'd, and so fairly won,
Came not till now to dignify the times
Since Cæsar's fortunes.
   North.   How is this deriv'd?
Saw you the field? came you from Shrewsbury?   24
   L. Bard. I spake with one, my lord, that came
      from thence;

3 attend: *await*   4 orchard: *garden*   13 an: *if*
19 brawn: *the fleshy part of the body, especially the buttocks or the
   calf of the leg*   21 follow'd: *carried through*

A gentleman well bred and of good name,
That freely render'd me these news for true.

    North. Here comes my servant Travers, whom I
    sent   28
On Tuesday last to listen after news.

    L. Bard. My lord, I over-rode him on the way;
And he is furnish'd with no certainties
More than he haply may retail from me.   32

Enter Travers.

    North. Now, Travers, what good tidings comes
    with you?

    Tra. My lord, Sir John Umfrevile turn'd me back
With joyful tidings; and, being better hors'd,
Out-rode me. After him came spurring hard   36
A gentleman, almost forspent with speed,
That stopp'd by me to breathe his bloodied horse.
He ask'd the way to Chester; and of him
I did demand what news from Shrewsbury.   40
He told me that rebellion had bad luck,
And that young Harry Percy's spur was cold.
With that he gave his able horse the head,
And, bending forward, struck his armed heels   44
Against the panting sides of his poor jade
Up to the rowel-head, and, starting so,
He seem'd in running to devour the way,
Staying no longer question.

    North.   Ha! Again: 48
Said he young Harry Percy's spur was cold?
Of Hotspur, Coldspur? that rebellion
Had met ill luck?

    L. Bard.   My lord, I'll tell you what:
If my young lord your son have not the day,   52

30 over-rode: *passed*   37 forspent: *exhausted*
43 able: *active*   48 Staying: *awaiting*   question: *talk*

Upon mine honour, for a silken point
I'll give my barony: never talk of it.
   North. Why should the gentleman that rode by
      Travers
Give then such instances of loss?
   L. Bard.   Who, he?   56
He was some hilding fellow that had stolen
The horse he rode on, and, upon my life,
Spoke at a venture. Look, here comes more news.

              Enter Morton.

   North. Yea, this man's brow, like to a title-leaf, 60
Foretells the nature of a tragic volume:
So looks the strond, whereon the imperious flood
Hath left a witness'd usurpation.
Say, Morton, didst thou come from Shrewsbury? 64
   Mor. I ran from Shrewsbury, my noble lord;
Where hateful death put on his ugliest mask
To fright our party.
   North.   How doth my son, and brother?
Thou tremblest, and the whiteness in thy cheek   68
Is apter than thy tongue to tell thy errand.
Even such a man, so faint, so spiritless,
So dull, so dead in look, so woe-begone,
Drew Priam's curtain in the dead of night,   72
And would have told him half his Troy was burn'd;
But Priam found the fire ere he his tongue,
And I my Percy's death ere thou report'st it.
This thou wouldst say, 'Your son did thus and thus; 76
Your brother thus; so fought the noble Douglas';
Stopping my greedy ear with their bold deeds:
But in the end, to stop mine ear indeed,
Thou hast a sigh to blow away this praise,   80

53 point: *lacing, garter*   57 hilding: *worthless*
62 strond: *shore*   63 witness'd usurpation: *traces of its usurpation*
69 apter: *more ready*

Ending with 'Brother, son, and all are dead.'

   Mor. Douglas is living, and your brother, yet;
But, for my lord your son,—

   North.   Why, he is dead.—
See, what a ready tongue suspicion hath!   84
He that but fears the thing he would not know
Hath by instinct knowledge from others' eyes
That what he fear'd is chanced. Yet speak, Morton:
Tell thou thy earl his divination lies,   88
And I will take it as a sweet disgrace
And make thee rich for doing me such wrong.

   Mor. You are too great to be by me gainsaid;
Your spirit is too true, your fears too certain.   92

   North. Yet, for all this, say not that Percy's dead.
I see a strange confession in thine eye:
Thou shak'st thy head, and hold'st it fear or sin
To speak a truth. If he be slain, say so;   96
The tongue offends not that reports his death:
And he doth sin that doth belie the dead,
Not he which says the dead is not alive.
Yet the first bringer of unwelcome news   100
Hath but a losing office, and his tongue
Sounds ever after as a sullen bell,
Remember'd knolling a departing friend.

   L. Bard. I cannot think, my lord, your son is
    dead.   104

   Mor. I am sorry I should force you to believe
That which I would to God I had not seen;
But these mine eyes saw him in bloody state,
Rendering faint quittance, wearied and out-
    breath'd,   108
To Harry Monmouth; whose swift wrath beat down
The never-daunted Percy to the earth,

---

87 is chanced: *has happened*   108 quittance: *return of blows*

From whence with life he never more sprung up.
In few, his death,—whose spirit lent a fire　　112
Even to the dullest peasant in his camp,—
Being bruited once, took fire and heat away
From the best-temper'd courage in his troops;
For from his metal was his party steel'd;　　116
Which once in him abated, all the rest
Turn'd on themselves, like dull and heavy lead:
And as the thing that's heavy in itself,
Upon enforcement flies with greatest speed,　　120
So did our men, heavy in Hotspur's loss,
Lend to this weight such lightness with their fear
That arrows fled not swifter toward their aim
Than did our soldiers, aiming at their safety,　　124
Fly from the field. Then was that noble Worcester
Too soon ta'en prisoner; and that furious Scot,
The bloody Douglas, whose well-labouring sword
Had three times slain the appearance of the king,　　128
'Gan vail his stomach, and did grace the shame
Of those that turn'd their backs; and in his flight,
Stumbling in fear, was took. The sum of all
Is, that the king hath won, and hath sent out　　132
A speedy power to encounter you, my lord,
Under the conduct of young Lancaster
And Westmoreland. This is the news at full.

　　North. For this I shall have time enough to
　　　　mourn.　　136
In poison there is physic; and these news,
Having been well, that would have made me sick,
Being sick, have in some measure made me well:
And as the wretch, whose fever-weaken'd joints,　　140

112 In few: *in short*　　　　114 bruited: *rumored*
116-118 *Cf. n.*　　　　　　　　128 *Cf. n.*
129 'Gan vail his stomach: *began to lower his arrogant spirit*
　　did grace: *reflected credit on, set in a good light*

Like strengthless hinges, buckle under life,
Impatient of his fit, breaks like a fire
Out of his keeper's arms, even so my limbs,
Weaken'd with grief, being now enrag'd with
    grief,   144
Are thrice themselves.   Hence, therefore, thou nice
    crutch!
A scaly gauntlet now, with joints of steel
Must glove this hand: and hence, thou sickly quoif!
Thou art a guard too wanton for the head   148
Which princes, flesh'd with conquest, aim to hit.
Now bind my brows with iron; and approach
The ragged'st hour that time and spite dare bring
To frown upon the enrag'd Northumberland!   152
Let heaven kiss earth! now let not nature's hand
Keep the wild flood confin'd! let order die!
And let this world no longer be a stage
To feed contention in a lingering act;   156
But let one spirit of the first-born Cain
Reign in all bosoms, that, each heart being set
On bloody courses, the rude scene may end,
And darkness be the burier of the dead!   160

    Tra. This strained passion doth you wrong, my
    lord.

    L. Bard. Sweet earl, divorce not wisdom from your
    honour.

    Mor. The lives of all your loving complices
Lean on your health; the which, if you give o'er 164
To stormy passion, must perforce decay.

141 buckle: *bend*   144 grief: *suffering*   grief: *sorrow*
145 nice: *dainty, effeminate*   147 sickly quoif: *sick man's hood*
148 wanton: *effeminate*
149 flesh'd: *made fierce by combat as a dog fed only on flesh*
151 ragged'st: *roughest*
161 strained passion: *exaggerated emotion*   163 complices: *allies*

You cast the event of war, my noble lord,
And summ'd the account of chance, before you said,
'Let us make head.'   It was your presurmise   168
That in the dole of blows your son might drop:
You knew he walk'd o'er perils, on an edge,
More likely to fall in than to get o'er;
You were advis'd his flesh was capable   172
Of wounds and scars, and that his forward spirit
Would lift him where most trade of danger rang'd:
Yet did you say, 'Go forth'; and none of this,
Though strongly apprehended, could restrain   176
The stiff-borne action: what hath then befallen,
Or what hath this bold enterprise brought forth,
More than that being which was like to be?

    L. Bard. We all that are engaged to this loss   180
Knew that we ventur'd on such dangerous seas
That if we wrought out life 'twas ten to one;
And yet we ventur'd, for the gain propos'd
Chok'd the respect of likely peril fear'd;   184
And since we are o'erset, venture again.
Come, we will all put forth, body and goods.

    Mor. 'Tis more than time: and, my most noble
      lord,
I hear for certain, and do speak the truth,   188
The gentle Archbishop of York is up,
With well-appointed powers: he is a man
Who with a double surety binds his followers.
My lord your son had only but the corpse,   192
But shadows and the shows of men to fight;
For that same word, rebellion, did divide
The action of their bodies from their souls;

166-179 *Cf. n.*   166 cast the event: *considered the outcome*
168 make head: *raise an army*   169 dole: *distribution*
170 edge: *dangerous narrow path*   172 advis'd: *aware*
177 stiff-borne: *obstinately carried out*
180 engaged to: *involved in*   184 respect: *consideration*
190 well-appointed: *well-equipped*

And they did fight with queasiness, constrain'd,   196
As men drink potions, that their weapons only
Seem'd on our side: but, for their spirits and souls,
This word, rebellion, it had froze them up,
As fish are in a pond. But now the bishop   200
Turns insurrection to religion:
Suppos'd sincere and holy in his thoughts,
He's follow'd both with body and with mind,
And doth enlarge his rising with the blood   204
Of fair King Richard, scrap'd from Pomfret stones;
Derives from heaven his quarrel and his cause;
Tells them he doth bestride a bleeding land,
Gasping for life under great Bolingbroke;   208
And more and less do flock to follow him.

    North. I knew of this before; but, to speak truth,
This present grief had wip'd it from my mind.
Go in with me; and counsel every man   212
The aptest way for safety and revenge:
Get posts and letters, and make friends with speed:
Never so few, and never yet more need.   *Exeunt.*

Scene Two

[*London. A Street*]

*Enter Sir John [Falstaff,] with his Page bearing his
sword and buckler.*

    Fal. Sirrah, you giant, what says the doctor
to my water?
    Page. He said, sir, the water itself was a good
healthy water; but, for the party that owed it,   4
he might have moe diseases than he knew for.

196 queasiness: *squeamishness*   204, 205 *Cf. n.*
204 enlarge: *widen the scope or appeal*   208 Bolingbroke; *cf. n.*
209 more and less: *high and low*   214 make: *collect*
4 owed: *owned*

Fal. Men of all sorts take a pride to gird at
me: the brain of this foolish-compounded clay,
man, is not able to invent anything that tends 8
to laughter, more than I invent or is invented
on me: I am not only witty in myself, but the
cause that wit is in other men. I do here walk
before thee like a sow that hath overwhelmed all 12
her litter but one. If the prince put thee into
my service for any other reason than to set me
off, why then I have no judgment. Thou whoreson mandrake, thou art fitter to be worn in my 16
cap than to wait at my heels. I was never
manned with an agate till now; but I will set
you neither in gold nor silver, but in vile apparel,
and send you back again to your master, for a 20
jewel; the juvenal, the prince your master, whose
chin is not yet fledged. I will sooner have a
beard grow in the palm of my hand than he shall
get one on his cheek; and yet he will not stick 24
to say, his face is a face-royal: God may finish it
when he will, it is not a hair amiss yet: he may
keep it still as a face-royal, for a barber shall
never earn sixpence out of it; and yet he'll 28
be crowing as if he had writ man ever since his
father was a bachelor. He may keep his own
grace, but he is almost out of mine, I can assure
him. What said Master Dombledon about the 32
satin for my short cloak and my slops?

Page. He said, sir, you should procure him
better assurance than Bardolph; he would not

6 gird: *jeer*
15 whoreson: *a coarse term of endearment (as here) or of contempt (as in l. 39)*
16 mandrake: *a poisonous plant whose forked root was supposed to
resemble the human form*   18 manned with an agate; *cf. n.*
21 juvenal: *used jocularly for 'youth'*   25 face-royal; *cf. n.*
29 writ man: *enrolled himself a man*   33 slops: *loose breeches*

take his bond and yours: he liked not the 36
security.

Fal. Let him be damned like the glutton! Pray
God his tongue be hotter! A whoreson Achitophel! a rascally yea-forsooth knave! to bear a 40
gentleman in hand, and then stand upon security.
The whoreson smooth-pates do now wear nothing but high shoes, and bunches of keys at their
girdles; and if a man is through with them in 44
honest taking up, then they must stand upon
security. I had as lief they would put ratsbane
in my mouth as offer to stop it with security. I
looked a' should have sent me two and twenty 48
yards of satin, as I am a true knight, and he
sends me security. Well, he may sleep in security; for he hath the horn of abundance, and the
lightness of his wife shines through it: and yet 52
cannot he see, though he have his own lanthorn
to light him. Where's Bardolph?

Page. He's gone into Smithfield to buy your
worship a horse.   56

Fal. I bought him in Paul's, and he'll buy
me a horse in Smithfield: an I could get me
but a wife in the stews, I were manned, horsed,
and wived.   60

Enter Chief Justice and Servant.

Page. Sir, here comes the nobleman that
committed the prince for striking him about
Bardolph.

Fal. Wait close; I will not see him.   64

38 glutton; *cf. n.*   39 Achitophel; *cf. n.*
40 yea-forsooth knave; *cf. n.*
   bear . . . in hand: *delude with false hopes*
42 smooth-pates: *round-heads, or Puritanical citizen class*
44 through: *serious*   45 taking up: *obtaining goods on trust*
48 a': *he*   51-54 *Cf. n.*   57 Paul's; *cf. n.*   61, 62 *Cf. n.*

Ch. Just. What's he that goes there?

Ser. Falstaff, an't please your lordship.

Ch. Just. He that was in question for the robbery?   68

Ser. He, my lord; but he hath since done good service at Shrewsbury, and, as I hear, is now going with some charge to the Lord John of Lancaster.   72

Ch. Just. What, to York? Call him back again.

Ser. Sir John Falstaff!

Fal. Boy, tell him I am deaf.   76

Page. You must speak louder, my master is deaf.

Ch. Just. I am sure he is, to the hearing of anything good. Go, pluck him by the elbow; I 80 must speak with him.

Ser. Sir John!

Fal. What! a young knave, and beg! Is there not wars? is there not employment? doth not 84 the king lack subjects? do not the rebels want soldiers? Though it be a shame to be on any side but one, it is worse shame to beg than to be on the worst side, were it worse than the name 88 of rebellion can tell how to make it.

Ser. You mistake me, sir.

Fal. Why, sir, did I say you were an honest man? setting my knighthood and my soldier- 92 ship aside, I had lied in my throat if I had said so.

Ser. I pray you, sir, then set your knighthood and your soldiership aside, and give me leave to 96

71 charge: *military command*

tell you you lie in your throat if you say I
am any other than an honest man.

Fal. I give thee leave to tell me so! I lay
aside that which grows to me! If thou gett'st 100
any leave of me, hang me: if thou takest leave,
thou wert better be hanged. You hunt counter:
hence! avaunt!

Ser. Sir, my lord would speak with you.   104

Ch. Just. Sir John Falstaff, a word with
you.

Fal. My good lord! God give your lordship
good time of day. I am glad to see your lord- 108
ship abroad; I heard say your lordship was sick:
I hope your lordship goes abroad by advice.
Your lordship, though not clean past your youth,
hath yet some smack of age in you, some relish 112
of the saltness of time; and I most humbly beseech your lordship to have a reverend care of
your health.

Ch. Just. Sir John, I sent for you before your 116
expedition to Shrewsbury.

Fal. An't please your lordship, I hear his
majesty is returned with some discomfort from
Wales.   120

Ch. Just. I talk not of his majesty. You
would not come when I sent for you.

Fal. And I hear, moreover, his highness is
fallen into this same whoreson apoplexy.   124

Ch. Just. Well, God mend him! I pray you,
let me speak with you.

Fal. This apoplexy is, as I take it, a kind of
lethargy, an't please your lordship; a kind of 128
sleeping in the blood, a whoreson tingling.

102 hunt counter; *cf. n.*

Ch. Just. What tell you me of it? be it as
it is.

Fal. It hath it original from much grief, 132
from study and perturbation of the brain.   I
have read the cause of his effects in Galen: it is
a kind of deafness.

Ch. Just. I think you are fallen into the dis- 136
ease, for you hear not what I say to you.

Fal. Very well, my lord, very well: rather,
an 't please you, it is the disease of not listening,
the malady of not marking, that I am troubled 140
withal.

Ch. Just. To punish you by the heels would
amend the attention of your ears; and I care
not if I do become your physician.   144

Fal. I am as poor as Job, my lord, but not so
patient: your lordship may minister the potion
of imprisonment to me in respect of poverty;
but how I should be your patient to follow your 148
prescriptions, the wise may make some dram of
a scruple, or indeed a scruple itself.

Ch. Just. I sent for you, when there were
matters against you for your life, to come speak 152
with me.

Fal. As I was then advised by my learned
counsel in the laws of this land-service, I did
not come.   156

Ch. Just. Well, the truth is, Sir John, you
live in great infamy.

Fal. He that buckles him in my belt cannot
live in less.   160

130 What: *why*   132 it: *its*   134 his: *its*
142 punish by the heels: *commit to prison; originally, to the stocks*
147 in respect of: *on account of*   155 land-service: *military service*

Ch. Just. Your means are very slender, and your waste is great.

Fal. I would it were otherwise: I would my means were greater and my waist slenderer.   164

Ch. Just. You have misled the youthful prince.

Fal. The young prince hath misled me: I am the fellow with the great belly, and he my dog.   168

Ch. Just. Well, I am loath to gall a new-healed wound: your day's service at Shrewsbury hath a little gilded over your night's exploit on Gadshill: you may thank the unquiet time for your 172 quiet o'er-posting that action.

Fal. My lord!

Ch. Just. But since all is well, keep it so: wake not a sleeping wolf.   176

Fal. To wake a wolf is as bad as to smell a fox.

Ch. Just. What! you are as a candle, the better part burnt out.   180

Fal. A wassail candle, my lord; all tallow: if I did say of wax, my growth would approve the truth.

Ch. Just. There is not a white hair on your 184 face but should have his effect of gravity.

Fal. His effect of gravy, gravy, gravy.

Ch. Just. You follow the young prince up and down, like his ill angel.   188

Fal. Not so, my lord; your ill angel is light, but I hope he that looks upon me will take me without weighing: and yet, in some respects, I grant, I cannot go, I cannot tell. Virtue is of 192

166-168 *Cf. n.*   173 o'er-posting: *getting over rapidly*
181 wassail candle: *large candle used at a feast*
182 wax; *cf. n.*   approve: *prove*
188 ill: *evil*   189-192 *Cf. n.*

so little regard in these costermonger times that
true valour is turned bear-herd: pregnancy is
made a tapster, and hath his quick wit wasted
in giving reckonings: all the other gifts apperti- 196
nent to man, as the malice of this age shapes
them, are not worth a gooseberry. You that are
old consider not the capacities of us that are
young; you measure the heat of our livers with 200
the bitterness of your galls; and we that are in
the vaward of our youth, I must confess, are
wags too.

Ch. Just. Do you set down your name in the 204
scroll of youth, that are written down old with
all the characters of age? Have you not a moist
eye, a dry hand, a yellow cheek, a white beard,
a decreasing leg, an increasing belly? Is not 208
your voice broken, your wind short, your chin
double, your wit single, and every part about
you blasted with antiquity, and will you yet call
yourself young? Fie, fie, fie, Sir John!   212

Fal. My lord, I was born about three of the
clock in the afternoon, with a white head, and
something a round belly. For my voice, I have
lost it with hollaing, and singing of anthems. 216
To approve my youth further, I will not: the
truth is, I am only old in judgment and under-
standing; and he that will caper with me for a
thousand marks, let him lend me the money, 220
and have at him! For the box o' the ear that
the prince gave you, he gave it like a rude prince,
and you took it like a sensible lord. I have

193 costermonger: *commercial*
194 bear-herd: *one who leads about a tame bear*
   pregnancy: *readiness of wit*   196 reckonings: *bills*
202 vaward: *vanguard*   210 single: *thin*
220 marks: *a mark was worth about thirteen shillings*

checked him for it, and the young lion repents; 224
marry, not in ashes and sackcloth, but in new
silk and old sack.

Ch. Just. Well, God send the prince a better
companion!   228

Fal. God send the companion a better prince!
I cannot rid my hands of him.

Ch. Just. Well, the king hath severed you
and Prince Harry. I hear you are going with 232
Lord John of Lancaster against the archbishop
and the Earl of Northumberland.

Fal. Yea; I thank your pretty sweet wit for
it. But look you pray, all you that kiss my lady 236
Peace at home, that our armies join not in a hot
day; for, by the Lord, I take but two shirts out
with me, and I mean not to sweat extraordinarily:
if it be a hot day, and I brandish anything but 240
my bottle, I would I might never spit white again.
There is not a dangerous action can peep out
his head but I am thrust upon it. Well, I cannot last ever. But it was always yet the trick of 244
our English nation, if they have a good thing, to
make it too common. If you will needs say I am
an old man, you should give me rest. I would
to God my name were not so terrible to the 248
enemy as it is: I were better to be eaten to death
with rust than to be scoured to nothing with
perpetual motion.

Ch. Just. Well, be honest, be honest; and 252
God bless your expedition.

Fal. Will your lordship lend me a thousand
pound to furnish me forth?

Ch. Just. Not a penny; not a penny; you are 256

too impatient to bear crosses.   Fare you well:
commend me to my cousin Westmoreland.

> [*Exeunt Chief Justice and Servant.*]

Fal. If I do, fillip me with a three-man beetle.
A man can no more separate age and covetous- 260
ness than a' can part young limbs and lechery;
but the gout galls the one, and the pox pinches
the other; and so both the degrees prevent my
curses.   Boy!   264

Page. Sir!

Fal. What money is in my purse?

Page. Seven groats and twopence.

Fal. I can get no remedy against this con- 268
sumption of the purse: borrowing only lingers
and lingers it out, but the disease is incurable.
Go bear this letter to my Lord of Lancaster;
this to the prince; this to the Earl of Westmore- 272
land; and this to old Mistress Ursula, whom I
have weekly sworn to marry since I perceived
the first white hair on my chin.   About it: you
know where to find me.   A pox of this gout! 276
or, a gout of this pox! for the one or the
other plays the rogue with my great toe.   'Tis
no matter if I do halt; I have the wars for my
colour, and my pension shall seem the more 280
reasonable.   A good wit will make use of anything; I will turn diseases to commodity.   *Exeunt.*

257 *Cf. n.*   259 *Cf. n.*   263 prevent: *anticipate*
267 groat: *a coin worth fourpence*   279 halt: *limp*
280 colour: *excuse*
282 commodity: *merchandise to be sold at a profit*

Scene Three

[*York.   The Archbishop's Palace*]

*Enter Archbishop, Hastings, Mowbray, and Lord
Bardolph.*

Arch. Thus have you heard our cause and known
    our means;
And, my most noble friends, I pray you all,
Speak plainly your opinions of our hopes:
And first, Lord Marshal, what say you to it?   4
    Mowb. I well allow the occasion of our arms;
But gladly would be better satisfied
How in our means we should advance ourselves
To look with forehead bold and big enough   8
Upon the power and puissance of the king.
    Hast. Our present musters grow upon the file
To five-and-twenty thousand men of choice;
And our supplies live largely in the hope   12
Of great Northumberland, whose bosom burns
With an incensed fire of injuries.
    L. Bard. The question, then, Lord Hastings, stand-
    eth thus:
Whether our present five-and-twenty thousand   16
May hold up head without Northumberland.
    Hast. With him, we may.
    L. Bard.   Ay, marry, there's the point:
But if without him we be thought too feeble,
My judgment is, we should not step too far   20
Till we had his assistance by the hand;
For in a theme so bloody-fac'd as this,
Conjecture, expectation, and surmise
Of aids incertain should not be admitted.   24

10 file: *muster roll*   12 supplies: *reinforcements*

Arch. 'Tis very true, Lord Bardolph; for, indeed
It was young Hotspur's case at Shrewsbury.

    L. Bard. It was, my lord; who lin'd himself with
      hope,
Eating the air on promise of supply,   28
Flattering himself with project of a power
Much smaller than the smallest of his thoughts;
And so, with great imagination
Proper to madmen, led his powers to death,   32
And winking leap'd into destruction.

    Hast. But, by your leave, it never yet did hurt
To lay down likelihoods and forms of hope.

    L. Bard. Yes, if this present quality of war,— 36
Indeed the instant action,—a cause on foot,
Lives so in hope, as in an early spring
We see the appearing buds; which, to prove fruit,
Hope gives not so much warrant as despair   40
That frosts will bite them. When we mean to build,
We first survey the plot, then draw the model;
And when we see the figure of the house,
Then must we rate the cost of the erection;   44
Which if we find outweighs ability,
What do we then but draw anew the model
In fewer offices, or at last desist
To build at all? Much more, in this great work,— 48
Which is almost to pluck a kingdom down
And set another up,—should we survey
The plot of situation and the model,
Consent upon a sure foundation,   52
Question surveyors, know our own estate,
How able such a work to undergo,
To weigh against his opposite; or else,

27 lin'd: *strengthened*
29, 30 project . . . smaller: *anticipation of an army actually much
    smaller*   33 winking: *with eyes closed*   36-41 *Cf. n.*
43 figure: *plan*   47 offices: *domestic quarters*   53-55 *Cf. n.*

We fortify in paper, and in figures,   56
Using the names of men instead of men:
Like one that draws the model of a house
Beyond his power to build it; who, half through,
Gives o'er and leaves his part-created cost   60
A naked subject to the weeping clouds,
And waste for churlish winter's tyranny.

    Hast. Grant that our hopes, yet likely of fair
      birth,
Should be still-born, and that we now possess'd   64
The utmost man of expectation;
I think we are a body strong enough,
Even as we are, to equal with the king.

    L. Bard. What! is the king but five-and-twenty
      thousand?   68

    Hast. To us no more; nay, not so much, Lord
      Bardolph.
For his divisions, as the times do brawl,
Are in three heads: one power against the French,
And one against Glendower; perforce, a third   72
Must take up us: so is the unfirm king
In three divided, and his coffers sound
With hollow poverty and emptiness.

    Arch. That he should draw his several strengths
      together   76
And come against us in full puissance,
Need not be dreaded.

    Hast.   If he should do so,
He leaves his back unarm'd, the French and Welsh
Baying him at the heels: never fear that.   80

    L. Bard. Who is it like should lead his forces
      hither?

    Hast. The Duke of Lancaster and Westmoreland;

60 part-created cost: *costly fragment*   62 churlish: *rough*
70 as . . . brawl: *as the turbulent times dictate*   81 like: *probable*

Against the Welsh, himself and Harry Monmouth:
But who is substituted 'gainst the French   84
I have no certain notice.
    Arch.   Let us on
And publish the occasion of our arms.
The commonwealth is sick of their own choice;
Their over-greedy love hath surfeited.   88
A habitation giddy and unsure
Hath he that buildeth on the vulgar heart.
O thou fond many! with what loud applause
Didst thou beat heaven with blessing Bolingbroke 92
Before he was what thou wouldst have him be:
And being now trimm'd in thine own desires,
Thou, beastly feeder, art so full of him
That thou provok'st thyself to cast him up.   96
So, so, thou common dog, didst thou disgorge
Thy glutton bosom of the royal Richard,
And now thou wouldst eat thy dead vomit up,
And howl'st to find it. What trust is in these
    times?   100
They that, when Richard liv'd, would have him die,
Are now become enamour'd on his grave:
Thou, that threw'st dust upon his goodly head,
When through proud London he came sighing on 104
After the admired heels of Bolingbroke,
Cry'st now, 'O earth! yield us that king again,
And take thou this!' O, thoughts of men accurst!
Past and to come seem best; things present worst. 108
    Mowb. Shall we go draw our numbers and set on?
    Hast. We are time's subjects, and time bids be
    gone.   [*Exeunt.*]

91 fond many: *foolish multitude*
94 trimm'd . . . desires: *supplied with what thou didst desire*
109 draw: *assemble*

ACT SECOND

Scene One

[*London. A Street*]

Enter Hostess [*Quickly of the Tavern*], *with two Officers, Fang and Snare.*

Host. Master Fang, have you entered the action?

Fang. It is entered.

Host. Where's your yeoman? Is't a lusty 4 yeoman? will a' stand to 't?

Fang. Sirrah!—where's Snare?

Host. O Lord, ay! good Master Snare.

Snare. Here, here. 8

Fang. Snare, we must arrest Sir John Falstaff.

Host. Yea, good Master Snare; I have entered him and all. 12

Snare. It may chance cost some of us our lives, for he will stab.

Host. Alas the day! take heed of him: he stabbed me in mine own house, and that most 16 beastly. In good faith, a' cares not what mischief he doth if his weapon be out: he will foin like any devil; he will spare neither man, woman, nor child. 20

Fang. If I can close with him I care not for his thrust.

Host. No, nor I neither: I'll be at your elbow. 24

4 yeoman: *sheriff's officer*   19 foin: *thrust (in fencing)*

Fang. An I but fist him once; an a' come but within my vice,—

Host. I am undone by his going; I warrant you, he's an infinitive thing upon my score. 28 Good Master Fang, hold him sure: good Master Snare, let him not 'scape. A' comes continuantly to Pie-corner—saving your manhoods—to buy a saddle; and he's indited to dinner to the Lub- 32 ber's Head in Lumbert Street, to Master Smooth's the silkman: I pray ye, since my exion is entered, and my case so openly known to the world, let him be brought in to his answer. A hundred 36 mark is a long one for a poor lone woman to bear; and I have borne, and borne, and borne; and have been fubbed off, and fubbed off, and fubbed off, from this day to that day, that it is a 40 shame to be thought on. There is no honesty in such dealing; unless a woman should be made an ass, and a beast, to bear every knave's wrong. Yonder he comes; and that arrant malmsey- 44 nose knave, Bardolph, with him. Do your offices, do your offices, Master Fang and Master Snare; do me, do me, do me your offices.

Enter Falstaff, and Bardolph.

Fal. How now! whose mare's dead? what's 48 the matter?

Fang. Sir John, I arrest you at the suit of Mistress Quickly.

Fal. Away, varlets! Draw, Bardolph: cut 52

26 vice: *figuratively, grip*
28 infinitive: *infinite (Dame Quickly's more obvious errors in speech are not, hereafter, glossed)*   upon my score: *in my debt*
32, 33 Lubber's . . . Street: *Libbard's, i.e., Leopard's, Head Inn, in Lombard Street*   34 exion: *Dame Quickly's error for 'action'*
37 one; *cf. n.*   39 fubbed: *fobbed, i.e., put off deceitfully*
44, 45 malmsey-nose: *red-nosed*

me off the villain's head; throw the quean in
the channel.

Host. Throw me in the channel! I'll throw
thee in the channel. Wilt thou? wilt thou? thou 56
bastardly rogue! Murder, murder! Ah, thou
honey-suckle villain! wilt thou kill God's officers
and the king's? Ah, thou honey-seed rogue!
thou art a honey-seed, a man-queller, and a 60
woman-queller.

Fal. Keep them off, Bardolph.

Fang. A rescue! a rescue!

Host. Good people, bring a rescue or two! 64
Thou wo't, wo't thou? thou wo't, wo't ta? do,
do, thou rogue! do, thou hemp-seed!

Fal. Away, you scullion! you rampallian!
you fustilarian! I'll tickle your catastrophe. 68

Enter Chief Justice.

Ch. Just. What is the matter? keep the peace
here, ho!

Host. Good my lord, be good to me! I beseech you, stand to me! 72

Ch. Just. How now, Sir John! what! are you
      brawling here?
Doth this become your place, your time and business?
You should have been well on your way to York.
Stand from him, fellow: wherefore hang'st upon
      him? 76

Host. O, my most worshipful lord, an't
please your grace, I am a poor widow of Eastcheap, and he is arrested at my suit.

Ch. Just. For what sum? 80

53 quean: *hussy*   54 channel: *kennel, i.e., gutter*
58 honey-suckle: *Dame Quickly's error for 'homicidal'*
59 honey-seed: *homicide*   60 man-queller: *man-killer*
65 wo't: *wouldst*   ta: *thou*   67, 68 *Cf. n.*

Host. It is more than for some, my lord; it
is for all I have. He hath eaten me out of
house and home; he hath put all my substance
into that fat belly of his: but I will have some of 84
it out again, or I will ride thee o' nights like the
mare.

Fal. I think I am as like to ride the mare if
I have any vantage of ground to get up.   88

Ch. Just. How comes this, Sir John? Fie!
what man of good temper would endure this
tempest of exclamation? Are you not ashamed
to enforce a poor widow to so rough a course to 92
come by her own?

Fal. What is the gross sum that I owe thee?

Host. Marry, if thou wert an honest man,
thyself and the money too. Thou didst swear 96
to me upon a parcel-gilt goblet, sitting in my
Dolphin-chamber, at the round table, by a sea-
coal fire, upon Wednesday in Wheeson week,
when the prince broke thy head for liking his 100
father to a singing-man of Windsor, thou didst
swear to me then, as I was washing thy wound,
to marry me and make me my lady thy wife.
Canst thou deny it? Did not goodwife Keech, 104
the butcher's wife, come in then and call me
gossip Quickly? coming in to borrow a mess of
vinegar; telling us she had a good dish of
prawns; whereby thou didst desire to eat some, 108
whereby I told thee they were ill for a green
wound? And didst thou not, when she was gone
down stairs, desire me to be no more so famili-

---

86 mare: *nightmare*   90 temper: *character*
97 parcel-gilt: *partly gilded*
98 sea-coal: *mineral coal (brought by boat from Newcastle)*
99 Wheeson: *Whitsun*   104 Keech: *literally 'a lump of fat'*
109 green: *fresh*

arity with such poor people; saying that ere 112
long they should call me madam? And didst
thou not kiss me and bid me fetch thee thirty
shillings? I put thee now to thy book-oath:
deny it if thou canst.   116

Fal. My lord, this is a poor mad soul; and
she says up and down the town that her eldest
son is like you. She hath been in good case,
and the truth is, poverty hath distracted her. 120
But for those foolish officers, I beseech you I
may have redress against them.

Ch. Just. Sir John, Sir John, I am well acquainted with your manner of wrenching the 124
true cause the false way. It is not a confident
brow, nor the throng of words that come with
such more than impudent sauciness from you,
can thrust me from a level consideration; you 128
have, as it appears to me, practised upon the
easy-yielding spirit of this woman, and made
her serve your uses both in purse and in person.

Host. Yea, in troth, my lord.   132

Ch. Just. Prithee, peace. Pay her the debt
you owe her, and unpay the villainy you have
done her: the one you may do with sterling
money, and the other with current repentance. 136

Fal. My lord, I will not undergo this sneap
without reply. You call honourable boldness
impudent sauciness: if a man will make curtsy,
and say nothing, he is virtuous. No, my lord, 140
my humble duty remembered, I will not be your
suitor: I say to you, I do desire deliverance from
these officers, being upon hasty employment in
the king's affairs.   144

119 case: *circumstances*   128 level: *steady*
136 current: *genuine, with pun upon 'sterling'*   137 sneap: *snub*

Ch. Just. You speak as having power to do wrong: but answer in the effect of your reputation, and satisfy the poor woman.

Fal. Come hither, hostess.   148

[*Taking her aside.*]

Enter Master Gower.

Ch. Just. Now, Master Gower! what news?

Gow. The king, my lord, and Harry Prince of Wales
Are near at hand: the rest the paper tells.

[*Gives a letter.*]

Fal. As I am a gentleman.   152

Host. Faith, you said so before.

Fal. As I am a gentleman. Come, no more words of it.

Host. By this heavenly ground I tread on, 156 I must be fain to pawn both my plate and the tapestry of my dining-chambers.

Fal. Glasses, glasses, is the only drinking: and for thy walls, a pretty slight drollery, or the 160 story of the Prodigal, or the German hunting in water-work, is worth a thousand of these bed-hangings and these fly-bitten tapestries. Let it be ten pound if thou canst. Come, an it were 164 not for thy humours, there's not a better wench in England. Go, wash thy face, and draw the action. Come, thou must not be in this humour with me; dost not know me? Come, come, I 168 know thou wast set on to this.

Host. Prithee, Sir John, let it be but twenty

145 *Cf. n.*   146 in the effect of: *in a manner suitable to*
159 *Cf. n.*   160 drollery: *humorous painting*
161 German hunting: *German hunting-scene*
162 water-work: *water colors*   165 humours: *caprices*
166 draw: *withdraw*

nobles: i' faith, I am loath to pawn my plate,
so God save me, la!   172

Fal. Let it alone; I'll make other shift:
you'll be a fool still.

Host. Well, you shall have it, though I pawn
my gown. I hope you'll come to supper. You'll 176
pay me all together?

Fal. Will I live? [*To Bardolph.*] Go, with
her, with her; hook on, hook on.

Host. Will you have Doll Tearsheet meet 180
you at supper?

Fal. No more words; let's have her.

> *Exeunt Hostess,* [*Bardolph, Page,*]
> *and Sergeant*[*s*].

Ch. Just. I have heard better news.

Fal. What's the news, my lord?   184

Ch. Just. Where lay the king last night?

Gow. At Basingstoke, my lord.

Fal. I hope, my lord, all's well: what is the
news, my lord?   188

Ch. Just. Come all his forces back?

Gow. No; fifteen hundred foot, five hundred horse,
Are march'd up to my Lord of Lancaster,
Against Northumberland and the archbishop.   192

Fal. Comes the king back from Wales, my noble
lord?

Ch. Just. You shall have letters of me presently.
Come, go along with me, good Master Gower.

Fal. My lord!   196

Ch. Just. What's the matter?

Fal. Master Gower, shall I entreat you with
me to dinner?

---

171 nobles: *gold coins worth about six shillings*
194 presently: *immediately*

Gow. I must wait upon my good lord here; 200
I thank you, good Sir John.

Ch. Just. Sir John, you loiter here too long,
being you are to take soldiers up in counties as
you go.　　　　204

Fal. Will you sup with me, Master Gower?

Ch. Just. What foolish master taught you
these manners, Sir John?

Fal. Master Gower, if they become me not, 208
he was a fool that taught them me.　This is the
right fencing grace, my lord; tap for tap, and
so part fair.

Ch. Just. Now the Lord lighten thee! thou 212
art a great fool.　　　　　　　　　　*Exeunt.*

Scene Two

[The Same]

Enter Prince Henry [and] Poins.

Prince. Before God, I am exceeding weary.

Poins. Is 't come to that?　I had thought
weariness durst not have attached one of so
high blood.　　　　4

Prince. Faith, it does me, though it discolours the complexion of my greatness to ac-
knowledge it.　Doth it not show vilely in me to
desire small beer?　　　　8

Poins. Why, a prince should not be so loosely
studied as to remember so weak a composition.

Prince. Belike then my appetite was not
princely got; for, by my troth, I do now re- 12

210 *Cf. n.*　　　　212 lighten: *enlighten, used quibblingly*
3 attached: *seized*
5 discolours the complexion of my greatness: *makes me blush*
10 studied: *inclined*

member the poor creature, small beer. But,
indeed, these humble considerations make me out
of love with my greatness. What a disgrace is
it to me to remember thy name, or to know 16
thy face to-morrow! or to take note how many
pair of silk stockings thou hast; *viz.* these, and
those that were thy peach-coloured ones! or to
bear the inventory of thy shirts; as, one for 20
superfluity, and another for use! But that the
tennis-court-keeper knows better than I, for it
is a low ebb of linen with thee when thou keepest
not racket there; as thou hast not done a great 24
while, because the rest of thy low-countries have
made a shift to eat up thy holland: and God
knows whether those that bawl out the ruins
of thy linen shall inherit his kingdom; but the 28
midwives say the children are not in the fault;
whereupon the world increases, and kindreds
are mightily strengthened.

Poins. How ill it follows, after you have 32
laboured so hard, you should talk so idly! Tell
me, how many good young princes would do
so, their fathers being so sick as yours at this
time is?   36

Prince. Shall I tell thee one thing, Poins?

Poins. Yes, faith, and let it be an excellent
good thing.

Prince. It shall serve among wits of no higher 40
breeding than thine.

Poins. Go to; I stand the push of your one
thing that you will tell.

Prince. Marry, I tell thee, it is not meet that 44
I should be sad, now my father is sick: albeit I

could tell to thee,—as to one it pleases me, for
fault of a better, to call my friend,—I could be
sad, and sad indeed too.   48

Poins. Very hardly upon such a subject.

Prince. By this hand, thou thinkest me as
far in the devil's book as thou and Falstaff for
obduracy and persistency: let the end try the 52
man. But I tell thee my heart bleeds inwardly
that my father is so sick; and keeping such vile
company as thou art hath in reason taken from
me all ostentation of sorrow.   56

Poins. The reason?

Prince. What wouldst thou think of me if I
should weep?

Poins. I would think thee a most princely 60
hypocrite.

Prince. It would be every man's thought;
and thou art a blessed fellow to think as every
man thinks: never a man's thought in the world 64
keeps the road-way better than thine: every man
would think me an hypocrite indeed. And what
accites your most worshipful thought to think so?

Poins. Why, because you have been so lewd 68
and so much engraffed to Falstaff.

Prince. And to thee.

Poins. By this light, I am well spoke on; I
can hear it with mine own ears: the worst that 72
they can say of me is that I am a second brother
and that I am a proper fellow of my hands; and
those two things I confess I cannot help. By the
mass, here comes Bardolph.   76

Enter Bardolph and Page.

67 accites: *invites*   68 lewd: *worthless*
69 much engraffed: *closely attached*   73 second brother: *younger son*
74 proper fellow of my hands: *good fellow with my fists*

Prince. And the boy that I gave Falstaff: a'
had him from me Christian; and look, if the fat
villain have not transformed him ape.

Bard. God save your Grace!   80

Prince. And yours, most noble Bardolph.

Poins. [*To the Page.*] Come, you virtuous ass,
you bashful fool, must you be blushing? wherefore blush you now? What a maidenly man-at- 84
arms are you become! Is 't such a matter to
get a pottle-pot's maidenhead?

Page. A' calls me even now, my lord, through
a red lattice, and I could discern no part of his 88
face from the window: at last, I spied his eyes,
and methought he had made two holes in the
ale-wife's new petticoat, and peeped through.

Prince. Hath not the boy profited?   92

Bard. Away, you whoreson upright rabbit,
away!

Page. Away, you rascally Althea's dream,
away!   96

Prince. Instruct us, boy; what dream, boy?

Page. Marry, my lord, Althea dreamed she
was delivered of a firebrand; and therefore I call
him her dream.   100

Prince. A crown's worth of good interpretation. There 'tis, boy.   [*Gives him money.*]

Poins. O! that this good blossom could be
kept from cankers. Well, there is sixpence to 104
preserve thee.

Bard. An you do not make him be hanged
among you, the gallows shall have wrong.

Prince. And how doth thy master, Bardolph? 108

86 pottle-pot: *two-quart tankard*   88 red lattice: *ale-house window*
95-100 *Cf. n.*   104 cankers: *canker-worms*

Bard. Well, my lord. He heard of your Grace's coming to town: there's a letter for you.

Poins. Delivered with good respect. And how doth the martlemas, your master?   112

Bard. In bodily health, sir.

Poins. Marry, the immortal part needs a physician; but that moves not him: though that be sick, it dies not.   116

Prince. I do allow this wen to be as familiar with me as my dog; and he holds his place, for look you how he writes.

Poins. [*looking over the Prince's shoulder.*]   120 'John Falstaff, knight,'—every man must know that, as oft as he has occasion to name himself: even like those that are kin to the king, for they never prick their finger but they say, 'There's   124 some of the king's blood spilt.' 'How comes that?' says he that takes upon him not to conceive. The answer is as ready as a borrower's cap, 'I am the king's poor cousin, sir.'   128

Prince. Nay, they will be kin to us, or they will fetch it from Japhet. But to the letter: 'Sir John Falstaff, knight, to the son of the king nearest his father, Harry Prince of   132 Wales, greeting.'

Poins. Why, this is a certificate.

Prince. Peace! 'I will imitate the honourable Romans in brevity:'   136

Poins. He sure means brevity in breath, short-winded.

Prince. 'I commend me to thee, I commend

---

112 martlemas; *cf. n.*   117 wen: *swelling, i.e., Falstaff*
126 takes upon him: *pretends*   conceive: *understand*
127, 128 borrower's cap; *cf. n.*
130 fetch it from Japhet: *trace kinship through Japhet, the son of Noah*
130 ff. *Cf. n.*

thee, and I leave thee. Be not too familiar with 140
Poins; for he misuses thy favours so much that
he swears thou art to marry his sister Nell. Re-
pent at idle times as thou mayest, and so farewell.

> 'Thine, by yea and no,—which is as 144
> much as to say, as thou usest him,
> *Jack Falstaff*, with my familiars;
> *John*, with my brothers and sisters,
> and *Sir John* with all Europe.'   148

Poins. My lord, I'll steep this letter in sack
and make him eat it.

Prince. That's to make him eat twenty of
his words. But do you use me thus, Ned? must 152
I marry your sister?

Poins. God send the wench no worse fortune!—but I never said so.

Prince. Well, thus we play the fools with the
time, and the spirits of the wise sit in the clouds 156
and mock us. Is your master here in London?

Bard. Yea, my lord.

Prince. Where sups he? doth the old boar
feed in the old frank?   160

Bard. At the old place, my lord, in Eastcheap.

Prince. What company?

Page. Ephesians, my lord, of the old church. 164

Prince. Sup any women with him?

Page. None, my lord, but old Mistress Quickly
and Mistress Doll Tearsheet.

Prince. What pagan may that be?   168

Page. A proper gentlewoman, sir, and a kins-
woman of my master's.

Prince. Even such kin as the parish heifers

160 frank: *sty*   164 Ephesians: *slang term for jolly fellow*

are to the town bull. Shall we steal upon them, 172
Ned, at supper?

Poins. I am your shadow, my lord; I'll
follow you.

Prince. Sirrah, you boy, and Bardolph; no 176
word to your master that I am yet come to
town: there's for your silence.   [*Gives money.*]

Bard. I have no tongue, sir.

Page. And for mine, sir, I will govern it.   180

Prince. Fare ye well; go. [*Exeunt Bardolph
and Page.*] This Doll Tearsheet should be some
road.

Poins. I warrant you, as common as the way
between Saint Albans and London.   185

Prince. How might we see Falstaff bestow
himself to-night in his true colours, and not
ourselves be seen?

Poins. Put on two leathern jerkins and
aprons, and wait upon him at his table as
drawers.   191

Prince. From a god to a bull! a heavy
descension! it was Jove's case. From a prince
to a prentice! a low transformation! that shall
be mine; for in every thing the purpose must
weigh with the folly. Follow me, Ned.   *Exeunt*

Scene Three

[*Warkworth. Before Northumberland's Castle*]

*Enter Northumberland, his wife, and the wife to
Harry Percy.*

North. I pray thee, loving wife, and gentle daughter,

186 bestow: *behave*   192, 193 *Cf. n.*

Give even way unto my rough affairs:
Put not you on the visage of the times,
And be like them to Percy troublesome.   4
    Lady N. I have given over, I will speak no more:
Do what you will; your wisdom be your guide.
    North. Alas! sweet wife, my honour is at pawn;
And, but my going, nothing can redeem it.   8
    Lady P. O! yet for God's sake, go not to these
      wars.
The time was, father, that you broke your word
When you were more endear'd to it than now;
When your own Percy, when my heart's dear
    Harry,   12
Threw many a northward look to see his father
Bring up his powers; but he did long in vain.
Who then persuaded you to stay at home?
There were two honours lost, yours and your son's: 16
For yours, the God of heaven brighten it!
For his, it stuck upon him as the sun
In the grey vault of heaven; and by his light
Did all the chivalry of England move   20
To do brave acts: he was indeed the glass
Wherein the noble youth did dress themselves:
He had no legs, that practis'd not his gait;
And speaking thick, which nature made his blemish, 24
Became the accents of the valiant;
For those that could speak low and tardily,
Would turn their own perfection to abuse,
To seem like him: so that, in speech, in gait,   28
In diet, in affections of delight,
In military rules, humours of blood,
He was the mark and glass, copy and book,
That fashion'd others. And him, O wondrous him! 32

11 endear'd: *bound*   24 thick: *fast*
29 affections of delight: *favorite pastimes*   30 blood: *disposition*

O miracle of men! him did you leave,—
Second to none, unseconded by you,—
To look upon the hideous god of war
In disadvantage; to abide a field   36
Where nothing but the sound of Hotspur's name
Did seem defensible: so you left him.
Never, O! never, do his ghost the wrong
To hold your honour more precise and nice   40
With others than with him: let them alone.
The marshal and the archbishop are strong:
Had my sweet Harry had but half their numbers,
To-day might I, hanging on Hotspur's neck,   44
Have talk'd of Monmouth's grave.

    North.   Beshrew your heart,
Fair daughter! you do draw my spirits from me
With new lamenting ancient oversights.
But I must go and meet with danger there,   48
Or it will seek me in another place,
And find me worse provided.

    Lady N.   O! fly to Scotland,
Till that the nobles and the armed commons
Have of their puissance made a little taste.   52

    Lady P. If they get ground and vantage of the
        king,
Then join you with them, like a rib of steel,
To make strength stronger; but, for all our loves,
First let them try themselves. So did your son;   56
He was so suffer'd: so came I a widow;
And never shall have length of life enough
To rain upon remembrance with mine eyes,
That it may grow and sprout as high as heaven,   60
For recordation to my noble husband.

---

38 defensible: *able to furnish defense*   40 nice: *scrupulous*
61 For recordation to: *in memory of*

North. Come, come, go in with me. 'Tis with my
    mind
As with the tide swell'd up unto his height,
That makes a still-stand, running neither way: 64
Fain would I go to meet the archbishop,
But many thousand reasons hold me back.
I will resolve for Scotland: there am I,
Till time and vantage crave my company.   68
                                    Exeunt.

Scene Four

[*London.   A Room in the Boar's Head Tavern, in
Eastcheap*]

Enter two Drawers [*Francis and another*].

First Draw. What the devil hast thou brought
there? apple-johns? thou knowest Sir John cannot endure an apple-john.

Sec. Draw. Mass, thou sayst true. The prince   4
once set a dish of apple-johns before him, and
told him there were five more Sir Johns; and,
putting off his hat, said, 'I will now take my
leave of these six dry, round, old withered   8
knights.' It angered him to the heart; but he
hath forgot that.

First Draw. Why then, cover, and set them
down: and see if thou canst find out Sneak's   12
noise; Mistress Tearsheet would fain hear some
music. Dispatch: the room where they supped
is too hot; they'll come in straight.

Sec. Draw. Sirrah, here will be the prince   16
and Master Poins anon; and they will put on

2 apple-johns: *apples that keep well but become very much shriveled*
11 cover: *set the table*   13 noise: *band of musicians*

two of our jerkins and aprons; and Sir John
must not know of it: Bardolph hath brought
word.   20

First Draw. By the mass, here will be old
utis: it will be an excellent stratagem.

Sec. Draw. I'll see if I can find out Sneak.

Exit.

Enter Hostess and Doll.

Host. I' faith, sweetheart, methinks now you 24
are in an excellent good temperality: your pul-
sidge beats as extraordinarily as heart would
desire; and your colour, I warrant you, is as
red as any rose; in good truth, la! But, i' faith, 28
you have drunk too much canaries, and that's
a marvellous searching wine, and it perfumes
the blood ere one can say, What's this? How
do you now?   32

Dol. Better than I was: hem!

Host. Why, that's well said; a good heart's
worth gold. Lo! here comes Sir John.

Enter Falstaff [singing].

Fal. 'When Arthur first in court'—Empty 36
the jordan.—[*Exit Drawer.*]—'And was a
worthy king.' How now, Mistress Doll!

Host. Sick of a calm: yea, good faith.

Fal. So is all her sect; an they be once in a 40
calm they are sick.

Dol. A pox damn you, you muddy rascal, is
that all the comfort you give me?

Fal. You make fat rascals, Mistress Doll.   44

21, 22 old utis: *rare sport*   36 *Cf. n.*
37 jordan: *chamber-pot*   39 calm: *mistake for 'qualm'*
40 sect: *sex*

Dol. I make them! gluttony and diseases make them; I make them not.

Fal. If the cook help to make the gluttony, you help to make the diseases, Doll: we 48 catch of you, Doll, we catch of you; grant that, my poor virtue, grant that.

Dol. Yea, joy, our chains and our jewels.

Fal. 'Your brooches, pearls, and owches':— 52 for to serve bravely is to come halting off, you know: to come off the breach with his pike bent bravely, and to surgery bravely; to venture upon the charged chambers bravely,— 56

Dol. Hang yourself, you muddy conger, hang yourself!

Host. By my troth, this is the old fashion; you two never meet but you fall to some discord: 60 you are both, i' good truth, as rheumatic as two dry toasts; you cannot one bear with another's confirmities. What the good-year! one must bear, and that must be you: you are the weaker 64 vessel, as they say, the emptier vessel.

Dol. Can a weak empty vessel bear such a huge full hogshead? there's a whole merchant's venture of Bordeaux stuff in him: you have not 68 seen a hulk better stuffed in the hold. Come, I'll be friends with thee, Jack: thou art going to the wars; and whether I shall ever see thee again or no, there is nobody cares. 72

Enter Drawer [Francis].

Fran. Sir, Ancient Pistol's below, and would speak with you.

52 *Cf. n.*   owches: *jewels*   56 chambers: *small cannon*
57 conger: *eel*   61 rheumatic: *error for 'splenetic'* (?)
63 good-year: *corruption of French 'goujere,' 'the pox'*
73 Ancient: *ensign or second lieutenant, Peto being Captain Falstaff's first lieutenant*

Dol. Hang him, swaggering rascal! let him
not come hither: it is the foul-mouthedest rogue 76
in England.

Host. If he swagger, let him not come here:
no, by my faith; I must live among my neigh-
bours; I'll no swaggerers: I am in good name 80
and fame with the very best. Shut the door;
there comes no swaggerers here: I have not
lived all this while to have swaggering now:
shut the door, I pray you.   84

Fal. Dost thou hear, hostess?

Host. Pray ye, pacify yourself, Sir John:
there comes no swaggerers here.

Fal. Dost thou hear? it is mine ancient.   88

Host. Tilly-fally, Sir John, ne'er tell me:
your ancient swaggerer comes not in my doors.
I was before Master Tisick, the debuty, t'other
day; and, as he said to me,—'twas no longer ago 92
than Wedesday last,—'I' good faith, neighbor
Quickly,' says he;—Master Dumbe, our minister,
was by then;—'Neighbour Quickly,' says he, 'receive those that are civil, for,' said he, 'you are in 96
an ill name'; now, a' said so, I can tell whereupon; 'for,' says he, 'you are an honest woman,
and well thought on; therefore take heed what
guests you receive: receive,' says he, 'no swag- 100
gering companions.' There comes none here:—
you would bless you to hear what he said. No,
I'll no swaggerers.

Fal. He's no swaggerer, hostess; a tame 104
cheater, i' faith; you may stroke him as gently
as a puppy greyhound: he'll not swagger with

a Barbary hen if her feathers turn back in any
show of resistance. Call him up, drawer.   108
                                    [*Exit Francis.*]

Host. Cheater, call you him? I will bar no
honest man my house, nor no cheater; but I do
not love swaggering, by my troth; I am the
worse, when one says swagger. Feel, masters, 112
how I shake; look you, I warrant you.

Dol. So you do, hostess.

Host. Do I? yea, in very truth, do I, an
'twere an aspen leaf: I cannot abide swaggerers. 116

Enter Ancient Pistol, and Bardolph and his boy.

Pist. God save you, Sir John!

Fal. Welcome, Ancient Pistol. Here, Pistol,
I charge you with a cup of sack: do you discharge upon mine hostess.   120

Pist. I will discharge upon her, Sir John,
with two bullets.

Fal. She is pistol-proof, sir; you shall hardly
offend her.   124

Host. Come, I'll drink no proofs nor no
bullets: I'll drink no more than will do me
good, for no man's pleasure, I.

Pist. Then to you, Mistress Dorothy; I will 128
charge you.

Dol. Charge me! I scorn you, scurvy companion. What! you poor, base, rascally, cheat-
ing, lack-linen mate! Away, you mouldy rogue, 132
away! I am meat for your master.

Pist. I know you, Mistress Dorothy.

Dol. Away, you cut-purse rascal! you filthy

107 Barbary hen: *a ken whose feathers naturally turn back*
130 companion: *a term of contempt*   132 mate: *fellow, 'chap'*

bung, away! By this wine, I'll thrust my knife 136
in your mouldy chaps an you play the saucy
cuttle with me. Away, you bottle-ale rascal!
you basket-hilt stale juggler, you! Since when,
I pray you, sir? God's light! with two points 140
on your shoulder? much!

Pist. God let me not live but I will murder
your ruff for this!

          [*Attacking her, and tearing her ruff.*]

Fal. No more, Pistol: I would not have you 144
go off here. Discharge yourself of our company,
Pistol.

Host. No, good captain Pistol; not here,
sweet captain.   149

Dol. Captain! thou abominable damned
cheater, art thou not ashamed to be called
captain? An captains were of my mind, they
would truncheon you out for taking their names 152
upon you before you have earned them. You
a captain, you slave! for what? for tearing a
poor whore's ruff in a bawdy-house? He a
captain! Hang him, rogue! He lives upon 156
mouldy stewed prunes and dried cakes. A
captain! God's light, these villains will make
the word captain as odious as the word 'occupy,'
which was an excellent good word before it was 160
ill sorted: therefore captains had need look to 't.

Bard. Pray thee, go down, good ancient.

Fal. Hark thee hither, Mistress Doll.

Pist. Not I; I tell thee what, Corporal Bar- 164

---

136 bung: *slang for 'sharper'*   137 chaps: *jaws*
138 cuttle: *slang for 'cutpurse'*
139 basket-hilt: *referring to the basket-shaped steel hand-guard on
     the hilt of Pistol's sword*
     juggler Since when, etc.: *a cant exclamation of scorn*
140 two points: *shoulder tags, mark of an army commission*
159 occupy; *cf. n.*

dolph; I could tear her. I'll be revenged of
her.

Page. Pray thee, go down.

Pist. I'll see her damned first; to Pluto's 168
damned lake, by this hand, to the infernal deep,
with Erebus and tortures vile also. Hold hook
and line, say I. Down, down, dogs! down faitors. Have we not Hiren here?   172

Host. Good Captain Peesel, be quiet; 'tis
very late, i' faith. I beseek you now, aggravate
your choler.

Pist. These be good humours, indeed! Shall pack-
horses,   176
And hollow pamper'd jades of Asia,
Which cannot go but thirty mile a day,
Compare with Cæsars, and with Cannibals,
And Trojan Greeks? nay, rather damn them with 180
King Cerberus; and let the welkin roar.
Shall we fall foul for toys?

Host. By my troth, captain, these are very
bitter words.   184

Bard. Be gone, good ancient: this will grow
to a brawl anon.

Pist. Die men like dogs! give crowns like
pins! Have we not Hiren here?   188

Host. O' my word, captain, there's none
such here. What the good-year! do you think
I would deny her? for God's sake! be quiet.

Pist. Then feed, and be fat, my fair Calipolis. 192
Come, give's some sack.
Si fortune me tormente, sperato me contento.
Fear we broadsides? no, let the fiend give fire:

---

171 faitors: *imposters*   172 Hiren; *cf. n.*
177, 178 *Cf. n.*   179 Cannibals: *blunder for 'Hannibals'*
182 toys: *trifles*   192 *Cf. n.*   194 *Cf. n.*

Give me some sack; and, sweetheart, lie thou there. 196
                              [*Laying down his sword.*]
Come we to full points here, and are *et ceteras* noth-
    ing?

Fal. Pistol, I would be quiet.

Pist. Sweet knight, I kiss thy neif. What!
we have seen the seven stars.   200

Dol. For God's sake, thrust him down stairs!
I cannot endure such a fustian rascal.

Pist. 'Thrust him down stairs!' know we not
Galloway nags?   204

Fal. Quoit him down, Bardolph, like a shove-
groat shilling: nay, an a' do nothing but speak
nothing, a' shall be nothing here.

Bard. Come, get you down stairs.   208

Pist. What! shall we have incision? Shall we
    imbrue?   [*Snatching up his sword.*]
Then death rock me asleep, abridge my doleful days!
Why then, let grievous, ghastly, gaping wounds
Untwine the Sisters Three! Come, Atropos, I
    say!   212

Host. Here's goodly stuff toward!

Fal. Give me my rapier, boy.

Dol. I pray thee, Jack, I pray thee, do not
draw.   216

Fal. Get you down stairs.   [*Drawing.*]

Host. Here's a goodly tumult! I'll forswear
keeping house, afore I'll be in these tirrits and
frights. So; murder, I warrant now. Alas, alas! 220
put up your naked weapons; put up your naked
weapons.   [*Exeunt Bardolph and Pistol.*]

197 full points: *a full stop*   199 neif: *fist*
200 seven stars: *the Pleiades*   202 fustian: *nonsensical*
204 Galloway nags: *small and inferior breed of horses*
205 Quoit: *pitch*   shove-groat; *cf. n.*   209 imbrue: *draw blood*
212 Sisters Three: *the Fates, Clotho, Lachesis, and Atropos*
213 toward: *at hand*   219 tirrits: *blunder for terrors (?)*

Dol. I pray thee, Jack, be quiet; the rascal's gone. Ah! you whoreson little valiant villain, 224 you!

Host. Are you not hurt i' the groin? methought a' made a shrewd thrust at your belly.

[*Enter Bardolph.*]

Fal. Have you turned him out o' doors?   228

Bard. Yea, sir: the rascal's drunk. You have hurt him, sir, i' the shoulder.

Fal. A rascal, to brave me!

Dol. Ah, you sweet little rogue, you! Alas, 232 poor ape, how thou sweatest! Come, let me wipe thy face; come on, you whoreson chops. Ah, rogue! i' faith, I love thee. Thou art as valorous as Hector of Troy, worth five of Agamemnon, 236 and ten times better than the Nine Worthies. Ah, villain!

Fal. A rascally slave! I will toss the rogue in a blanket.   240

Dol. Do, an thou darest for thy heart: an thou dost, I'll canvass thee between a pair of sheets.

Enter Music.

Page. The music is come, sir.   244

Fal. Let them play. Play, sirs. Sit on my knee, Doll. A rascal bragging slave! the rogue fled from me like quicksilver.

Dol. I' faith, and thou followedst him like a 248 church. Thou whoreson little tidy Bartholomew boar-pig, when wilt thou leave fighting o' days,

234 chops: *fat-face*
249, 250 Bartholomew boar-pig: *roast pig, a favorite dish at Bartholo-mew Fair*

and foining o' nights, and begin to patch up
thine old body for heaven?   252

*Enter [behind] the Prince and Poins, disguised
[like Drawers].*

Fal. Peace, good Doll! do not speak like a
death's head: do not bid me remember mine
end.

Dol. Sirrah, what humour's the prince of? 256

Fal. A good shallow young fellow: a' would
have made a good pantler, a' would have chipped
bread well.

Dol. They say, Poins has a good wit.   260

Fal. He a good wit! hang him, baboon! his
wit is as thick as Tewksbury mustard: there is
no more conceit in him than is in a mallet.

Dol. Why does the prince love him so, then? 264

Fal. Because their legs are both of a bigness,
and a' plays at quoits well, and eats conger and
fennel, and drinks off candles' ends for flapdragons, and rides the wild mare with the boys, 268
and jumps upon joint-stools, and swears with a
good grace, and wears his boots very smooth,
like unto the sign of the leg, and breeds no bate
with telling of discreet stories; and such other 272
gambol faculties a' has, that show a weak mind
and an able body, for the which the prince
admits him: for the prince himself is such
another; the weight of a hair will turn the 276
scales between their avoirdupois.

258 pantler: *servant in charge of the pantry*
263 conceit: *imagination*   267 drinks . . . flapdragons; *cf. n.*
268 rides . . . mare: *plays see-saw*
269 joint-stools: *stools made by a joiner, as distinguished from those
       of rough make*
271 sign of the leg: *a shoemaker's sign*
    breeds no bate: *causes no strife*   273 gambol: *sportive*

Prince. Would not this nave of a wheel have his ears cut off?

Poins. Let's beat him before his whore. 280

Prince. Look, whether the withered elder hath not his poll clawed like a parrot.

Poins. Is it not strange that desire should so many years outlive performance?   284

Fal. Kiss me, Doll.

Prince. Saturn and Venus this year in conjunction! what says the almanack to that?

Poins. And, look, whether the fiery Trigon, 288 his man, be not lisping to his master's old tables, his note-book, his counsel-keeper.

Fal. Thou dost give me flattering busses.

Dol. By my troth, I kiss thee with a most 292 constant heart.

Fal. I am old, I am old.

Dol. I love thee better than I love e'er a scurvy young boy of them all.   296

Fal. What stuff wilt have a kirtle of? I shall receive money o' Thursday; shalt have a cap to-morrow. A merry song! come: it grows late; we'll to bed. Thou'lt forget me when I 300 am gone.

Dol. By my troth, thou'lt set me a-weeping an thou sayst so: prove that ever I dress myself handsome till thy return. Well, hearken at the 304 end.

Fal. Some sack, Francis!

Prince. ⎱ [*Coming forward.*] Anon, anon,
Poins. ⎰ sir.   308

278 nave of a wheel: *Falstaff's knavery and rotundity are both in-
    cluded in this phrase*   282 poll: *head*   286 *Cf. n.*
288 fiery Trigon: *Bardolph; cf. n.*
289 lisping: *making love*
    old tables: *old account book, i.e., the hostess*
297 kirtle: *waist or skirt or both*   304 hearken at: *watch*

Fal. Ha! a bastard son of the king's? And art not thou Poins his brother?

Prince. Why, thou globe of sinful continents, what a life dost thou lead!   312

Fal. A better than thou: I am a gentleman; thou art a drawer.

Prince. Very true, sir; and I come to draw you out by the ears.   316

Host. O! the Lord preserve thy good Grace; by my troth, welcome to London. Now, the Lord bless that sweet face of thine! O Jesu! are you come from Wales?   320

Fal. Thou whoreson mad compound of majesty, by this light flesh and corrupt blood [*pointing to Doll*], thou art welcome.

Dol. How, you fat fool! I scorn you.   324

Poins. My lord, he will drive you out of your revenge and turn all to a merriment, if you take not the heat.

Prince. You whoreson candle-mine, you, how 328 vilely did you speak of me even now before this honest, virtuous, civil gentlewoman!

Host. God's blessing of your good heart! and so she is, by my troth.   332

Fal. Didst thou hear me?

Prince. Yea; and you knew me, as you did when you ran away by Gadshill: you knew I was at your back, and spoke it on purpose to try 336 my patience.

Fal. No, no, no; not so; I did not think thou wast within hearing.

Prince. I shall drive you then to confess the 340

326, 327 take . . . the heat: *strike while the iron's hot*
328 candle-mine: *mine of tallow*

wilful abuse; and then I know how to handle
you.

Fal. No abuse, Hal, o' mine honour; no
abuse.   344

Prince. Not to dispraise me, and call me
pantler and bread-chipper and I know not what?

Fal. No abuse, Hal.

Poins. No abuse!   348

Fal. No abuse, Ned, in the world; honest
Ned, none. I dispraised him before the wicked,
that the wicked might not fall in love with him;
in which doing I have done the part of a careful 352
friend and a true subject, and thy father is to
give me thanks for it. No abuse, Hal; none,
Ned, none: no, faith, boys, none.

Prince. See now, whether pure fear and 356
entire cowardice doth not make thee wrong this
virtuous gentlewoman to close with us? Is she
of the wicked? Is thine hostess here of the
wicked? Or is thy boy of the wicked? Or 360
honest Bardolph, whose zeal burns in his nose, of
the wicked?

Poins. Answer, thou dead elm, answer.

Fal. The fiend hath pricked down Bardolph 364
irrecoverable; and his face is Lucifer's privy-
kitchen, where he doth nothing but roast malt-
worms. For the boy, there is a good angel about
him; but the devil outbids him too.   368

Prince. For the women?

Fal. For one of them, she is in hell already,
and burns poor souls. For the other, I owe her
money; and whether she be damned for that, I 372
know not.

358 close: *make peace*   363 dead elm; *cf. n.*
364 pricked down: *marked down*   366, 367 malt-worms: *ale-topers*

Host. No, I warrant you.

Fal. No, I think thou art not; I think thou art quit for that. Marry, there is another in- 376 dictment upon thee, for suffering flesh to be eaten in thy house, contrary to the law; for the which I think thou wilt howl.

Host. All victuallers do so: what's a joint of 380 mutton or two in a whole Lent?

Prince. You, gentlewoman,—

Dol. What says your Grace?

Fal. His Grace says that which his flesh 384 rebels against.

　　　　　　　　　　　　Peto knocks at door.

Host. Who knocks so loud at door? Look to the door there, Francis.

Enter Peto.

Prince. Peto, how now! what news?　　　388

Peto. The king your father is at Westminster;
And there are twenty weak and wearied posts
Come from the north: and as I came along,
I met and overtook a dozen captains,　　　392
Bare-headed, sweating, knocking at the taverns,
And asking every one for Sir John Falstaff.

Prince. By heaven, Poins, I feel me much to blame,
So idly to profane the precious time,　　　396
When tempest of commotion, like the south,
Borne with black vapour, doth begin to melt
And drop upon our bare unarmed heads.
Give me my sword and cloak. Falstaff, good night.　　　400

　　　Exeunt Prince and Poins [*Bardolph and Peto*].

376 quit: *absolved*　　　390 posts: *couriers*　　　397 south: *south wind*

Fal. Now comes in the sweetest morsel of the night, and we must hence and leave it un-picked. [*Knocking within.*] More knocking at the door!   404

[*Enter Bardolph.*]

How now! what's the matter?

Bard. You must away to court, sir, presently; A dozen captains stay at door for you.

Fal. [*To the Page*]. Pay the musicians, sirrah. 408 Farewell, hostess, farewell, Doll. You see, my good wenches, how men of merit are sought after: the undeserver may sleep when the man of action is called on. Farewell, good wenches. 412 If I be not sent away post, I will see you again ere I go.

Dol. I cannot speak; if my heart be not ready to burst,—well, sweet Jack, have a care 416 of thyself.

Fal. Farewell, farewell.

Exit [*Falstaff, with Bardolph*].

Host. Well, fare thee well: I have known thee these twenty-nine years, come peascod- 420 time; but an honester, and truer-hearted man, —well, fare thee well.

Bard. [*Within.*] Mistress Tearsheet!

Host. What's the matter?   424

Bard. [*Within.*] Bid Mistress Tearsheet come to my master.

Host. O! run, Doll, run; run, good Doll. Come!   *She comes blubbered.* 428 Yea, will you come, Doll?   *Exeunt.*

423 post: *in haste*   428 S. d. blubbered: *in tears*

ACT THIRD

Scene One

[Westminster. The Palace]

Enter the King in his night-gown, with a Page.

King. Go, call the Earls of Surrey and of War-
    wick;
But, ere they come, bid them o'er-read these letters,
And well consider of them. Make good speed.
                     [Exit Page.]
How many thousand of my poorest subjects   4
Are at this hour asleep! O sleep! O gentle sleep!
Nature's soft nurse, how have I frighted thee,
That thou no more wilt weigh my eyelids down
And steep my senses in forgetfulness?   8
Why rather, sleep, liest thou in smoky cribs,
Upon uneasy pallets stretching thee,
And hush'd with buzzing night-flies to thy slumber,
Than in the perfum'd chambers of the great,   12
Under the canopies of costly state,
And lull'd with sound of sweetest melody?
O thou dull god! why liest thou with the vile
In loathsome beds, and leav'st the kingly couch   16
A watch-case or a common 'larum bell?
Wilt thou upon the high and giddy mast
Seel up the ship-boy's eyes, and rock his brains
In cradle of the rude imperious surge,   20
And in the visitation of the winds,
Who take the ruffian billows by the top,
Curling their monstrous heads, and hanging them
With deaf'ning clamour in the slippery clouds,   24

S. d. night-gown: *dressing gown*
17 watch-case: *sentry-box*   19 Seel: *sew together (a hawking term)*

That with the hurly death itself awakes?
Canst thou, O partial sleep! give thy repose
To the wet sea-boy in an hour so rude,
And in the calmest and most stillest night,   28
With all appliances and means to boot,
Deny it to a king? Then, happy low, lie down!
Uneasy lies the head that wears a crown.

Enter Warwick and Surrey.

War. Many good morrows to your majesty!   32
King. Is it good morrow, lords?
War. 'Tis one o'clock, and past.
King. Why then, good morrow to you all, my lords.
Have you read o'er the letters that I sent you?   36
War. We have, my liege.
King. Then you perceive the body of our kingdom,
How foul it is; what rank diseases grow,
And with what danger, near the heart of it.   40
War. It is but as a body, yet distemper'd,
Which to his former strength may be restor'd
With good advice and little medicine:
My Lord Northumberland will soon be cool'd.   44
King. O God! that one might read the book of
          fate,
And see the revolution of the times
Make mountains level, and the continent,—
Weary of solid firmness,—melt itself   48
Into the sea! and, other times, to see
The beachy girdle of the ocean
Too wide for Neptune's hips; how chances mock,
And changes fill the cup of alteration   52
With divers liquors! O! if this were seen,
The happiest youth, viewing his progress through,
What perils past, what crosses to ensue,
25 hurly: *tumult*

Would shut the book, and sit him down and die.   56
'Tis not ten years gone
Since Richard and Northumberland, great friends,
Did feast together, and in two years after
Were they at wars: it is but eight years since   60
This Percy was the man nearest my soul,
Who like a brother toil'd in my affairs
And laid his love and life under my foot;
Yea, for my sake, even to the eyes of Richard   64
Gave him defiance. But which of you was by,—
[*To Warwick.*] You, cousin Nevil, as I may remem-
     ber,—
When Richard, with his eye brimful of tears,
Then check'd and rated by Northumberland,   68
Did speak these words, now prov'd a prophecy?
'Northumberland, thou ladder, by the which
My cousin Bolingbroke ascends my throne';
Though then, God knows, I had no such intent,   72
But that necessity so bow'd the state
That I and greatness were compelled to kiss:
'The time shall come,' thus did he follow it,
'The time will come, that foul sin, gathering head,   76
Shall break into corruption':—so went on,
Foretelling this same time's condition
And the division of our amity.

   War. There is a history in all men's lives,   80
Figuring the nature of the times deceas'd;
The which observ'd, a man may prophesy,
With a near aim, of the main chance of things
As yet not come to life, which in their seeds   84
And weak beginnings lie intreasured.
Such things become the hatch and brood of time;
And by the necessary form of this

68 check'd: *rebuked*   81 Figuring: *symbolizing*
87 necessary form: *logical necessity*

King Richard might create a perfect guess   88
That great Northumberland, then false to him,
Would of that seed grow to a greater falseness,
Which should not find a ground to root upon,
Unless on you.

    King.   Are these things then necessities? 92
Then let us meet them like necessities;
And that same word even now cries out on us.
They say the bishop and Northumberland
Are fifty thousand strong.

    War.   It cannot be, my lord! 96
Rumour doth double, like the voice and echo,
The numbers of the fear'd. Please it your Grace
To go to bed: upon my soul, my lord,
The powers that you already have sent forth   100
Shall bring this prize in very easily.
To comfort you the more, I have receiv'd
A certain instance that Glendower is dead.
Your majesty hath been this fortnight ill,   104
And these unseason'd hours perforce must add
Unto your sickness.

    King.   I will take your counsel:
And were these inward wars once out of hand,
We would, dear lords, unto the Holy Land.   108

                              Exeunt.

Scene Two

[*Before Justice Shallow's House in Gloucestershire*]

*Enter Shallow and Silence, with Mouldy, Shadow,
Wart, Feeble, Bullcalf [and Servants].*

    Shal. Come on, come on, come on, sir; give
me your hand, sir, give me your hand, sir: an

103 instance: *proof*   105 unseason'd: *unseasonable*

early stirrer, by the rood! And how doth my
good cousin Silence?   4

Sil. Good morrow, good cousin Shallow.

Shal. And how doth my cousin, your bedfellow? and your fairest daughter and mine, my
god-daughter Ellen?   8

Sil. Alas! a black ousel, cousin Shallow!

Shal. By yea and nay, sir, I dare say my
cousin William is become a good scholar. He is
at Oxford still, is he not?   12

Sil. Indeed, sir, to my cost.

Shal. A' must, then, to the inns o' court
shortly. I was once of Clement's Inn; where I
think they will talk of mad Shallow yet.   16

Sil. You were called 'lusty Shallow' then,
cousin.

Shal. By the mass, I was called anything;
and I would have done anything indeed too, 20
and roundly too. There was I, and Little John
Doit of Staffordshire, and black George Barnes,
and Francis Pickbone, and Will Squele a Cots-
wold man; you had not four such swinge-buck- 24
lers in all the inns o' court again: and, I may say
to you, we knew where the *bona-robas* were,
and had the best of them all at commandment.
Then was Jack Falstaff, now Sir John, a boy, and 28
page to Thomas Mowbray, Duke of Norfolk.

Sil. This Sir John, cousin, that comes hither
anon about soldiers?

Shal. The same Sir John, the very same. I 32
occ him break Skogan's head at the court gate,
when a' was a crack not thus high: and the very

---

3 rood: *cross*   9 ousel: *blackbird*
14 inns o' court: *colleges of law*   21 roundly: *thoroughly*
24 swinge-bucklers: *roisterers*   26 bona-robas: *showy harlots*
28, 29 *Cf. n.*   33 Skogan; *cf. n.*   34 crack: *lively youngster*

same day did I fight with one Sampson Stock-
fish, a fruiterer, behind Gray's Inn. Jesu! Jesu! 36
the mad days that I have spent; and to see how
many of my old acquaintance are dead!

Sil. We shall all follow, cousin.

Shal. Certain, 'tis certain; very sure, very 40
sure: death, as the Psalmist saith, is certain to
all; all shall die. How a good yoke of bullocks
at Stamford fair?

Sil. By my troth, I was not there.   44

Shal. Death is certain. Is old Double of your
town living yet?

Sil. Dead, sir.

Shal. Jesu! Jesu! dead! a' drew a good 48
bow; and dead! a' shot a fine shoot: John a
Gaunt loved him well, and betted much money
on his head. Dead! a' would have clapped i' the
clout at twelve score; and carried you a fore- 52
hand shaft a fourteen and fourteen and a half,
that it would have done a man's heart good to
see. How a score of ewes now?

Sil. Thereafter as they be: a score of good 56
ewes may be worth ten pounds.

Shal. And is old Double dead?

Sil. Here come two of Sir John Falstaff's
men, as I think.   60

Enter Bardolph, and his Boy.

Shal. Good morrow, honest gentlemen.

Bard. I beseech you, which is Justice Shallow?

Shal. I am Robert Shallow, sir; a poor
esquire of this county, and one of the king's 64

42 How: *what price*
51 clapped i' the clout: *hit the white mark in the target*
52 at twelve score: *at twelve score yards*
52, 53 forehand shaft: *arrow made for shooting straight forward*
53 a fourteen, etc.: *fourteen score yards*

justices of the peace: what is your good pleasure
with me?

Bard. My captain, sir, commends him to you;
my captain, Sir John Falstaff: a tall gentleman, 68
by heaven, and a most gallant leader.

Shal. He greets me well, sir. I knew him a
good backsword man. How doth the good
knight? may I ask how my lady his wife doth? 72

Bard. Sir, pardon; a soldier is better accommodated than with a wife.

Shal. It is well said, in faith, sir; and it is
well said indeed too. 'Better accommodated!' 76
it is good; yea indeed, is it: good phrases are
surely and ever were, very commendable. Accommodated! it comes of *accommodo:* very
good; a good phrase.   80

Bard. Pardon me, sir; I have heard the
word. 'Phrase,' call you it? By this good day,
I know not the phrase; but I will maintain the
word with my sword to be a soldier-like word, 84
and a word of exceeding good command, by
heaven. Accommodated; that is, when a man
is, as they say, accommodated; or, when a man
is, being, whereby, a' may be thought to be 88
accommodated, which is an excellent thing.

Enter Falstaff.

Shal. It is very just. Look, here comes good
Sir John. Give me your good hand, give me
your worship's good hand. By my truth, you 92
look well and bear your years very well: welcome, good Sir John.

---

68 tall: *doughty*   71 backsword man: *fighter at single-sticks*
73 accommodated; *cf. n.*

Fal. I am glad to see you well, good Master Robert Shallow. Master Surecard, as I think. 96

Shal. No, Sir John; it is my cousin, Silence, in commission with me.

Fal. Good Master Silence, it well befits you should be of the peace.   100

Sil. Your good worship is welcome.

Fal. Fie! this is hot weather, gentlemen. Have you provided me here half a dozen sufficient men?   104

Shal. Marry, have we, sir. Will you sit?

Fal. Let me see them, I beseech you.

Shal. Where's the roll? where's the roll? where's the roll? Let me see, let me see, 108 So, so, so, so, so, so, so: yea, marry, sir: Ralph Mouldy! let them appear as I call; let them do so, let them do so. Let me see; where is Mouldy?

Moul. Here, an't please you.   112

Shal. What think you, Sir John? a good-limbed fellow; young, strong, and of good friends.

Fal. Is thy name Mouldy?   116

Moul. Yea, an't please you.

Fal. 'Tis the more time thou wert used.

Shal. Ha, ha, ha! most excellent, i' faith! things that are mouldy lack use: very singular 120 good. In faith, well said, Sir John; very well said.

Fal. Prick him.

Moul. I was pricked well enough before, an 124 you could have let me alone: my old dame will be undone now for one to do her husbandry and

96 Surecard: *the name signifies 'boon companion'*
98 commission: *office*   104 sufficient: *fit*
123 Prick: *mark down*

her drudgery: you need not to have pricked me;
there are other men fitter to go out than I.   128

Fal. Go to: peace, Mouldy! you shall go.
Mouldy, it is time you were spent.

Moul. Spent!

Shal. Peace, fellow, peace! stand aside: know 132
you where you are? For the other, Sir John:
let me see. Simon Shadow!

Fal. Yea, marry, let me have him to sit
under: he's like to be a cold soldier.   136

Shal. Where's Shadow?

Shad. Here, sir.

Fal. Shadow, whose son art thou?

Shad. My mother's son, sir.   140

Fal. Thy mother's son! like enough, and thy
father's shadow: so the son of the female is the
shadow of the male: it is often so, indeed; but
not of the father's substance.   144

Shal. Do you like him, Sir John?

Fal. Shadow will serve for summer; prick
him, for we have a number of shadows to fill up
the muster-book.   148

Shal. Thomas Wart?

Fal. Where's he?

Wart. Here, sir.

Fal. Is thy name Wart?   152

Wart. Yea, sir.

Fal. Thou art a very ragged wart.

Shal. Shall I prick him, Sir John?

Fal. It were superfluous; for his apparel is 156
built upon his back, and the whole frame stands
upon pins: prick him no more.

147 shadows: *names, for which we receive pay, though we have not
the men*

Shal. Ha, ha, ha! you can do it, sir; you can do it: I commend you well. Francis Feeble!   160

Fee. Here, sir.

Fal. What trade art thou, Feeble?

Fee. A woman's tailor, sir.

Shal. Shall I prick him, sir?   164

Fal. You may; but if he had been a man's tailor he'd have pricked you. Wilt thou make as many holes in an enemy's battle as thou hast done in a woman's petticoat?   168

Fee. I will do my good will, sir: you can have no more.

Fal. Well said, good woman's tailor! well said, courageous Feeble! Thou wilt be as valiant 172 as the wrathful dove or most magnanimous mouse. Prick the woman's tailor; well, Master Shallow; deep, Master Shallow.

Fee. I would Wart might have gone, sir.   176

Fal. I would thou wert a man's tailor, that thou mightst mend him, and make him fit to go. I cannot put him to a private soldier that is the leader of so many thousands: let that 180 suffice, most forcible Feeble.

Fee. It shall suffice, sir.

Fal. I am bound to thee, reverend Feeble. Who is next?   184

Shal. Peter Bullcalf o' the green!

Fal. Yea, marry, let's see Bullcalf.

Bull. Here, sir.

Fal. 'Fore God, a likely fellow! Come, prick 188 me Bullcalf till he roar again.

Bull. O Lord! good my lord captain,—

Fal. What! dost thou roar before thou art pricked?   192

167 battle: *army*   180 thousands: *i.e., vermin*

Bull. O Lord, sir! I am a diseased man.

Fal. What disease hast thou?

Bull. A whoreson cold, sir; a cough, sir, which I caught with ringing in the king's affairs 196 upon his coronation day, sir.

Fal. Come, thou shalt go to the wars in a gown; we will have away thy cold; and I will take such order that thy friends shall ring for 200 thee. Is here all?

Shal. Here is two more called than your number; you must have but four here, sir: and so, I pray you, go in with me to dinner.   204

Fal. Come, I will go drink with you, but I cannot tarry dinner. I am glad to see you, by my troth, Master Shallow.

Shal. O, Sir John, do you remember since we 208 lay all night in the windmill in Saint George's field?

Fal. No more of that, good Master Shallow, no more of that.   212

Shal. Ha! 'twas a merry night. And is Jane Nightwork alive?

Fal. She lives, Master Shallow.

Shal. She never could away with me.   216

Fal. Never, never; she would always say she could not abide Master Shallow.

Shal. By the mass, I could anger her to the heart. She was then a *bona-roba.* Doth she 220 hold her own well?

Fal. Old, old, Master Shallow.

Shal. Nay, she must be old; she cannot choose but be old; certain she's old; and had Robin 224

200 such order: *such measures*   216 away with: *endure*

Nightwork by old Nightwork before I came to
Clement's Inn.

Sil. That's fifty-five years ago.

Shal. Ha! cousin Silence, that thou hadst 228
seen that that this knight and I have seen. Ha!
Sir John, said I well?

Fal. We have heard the chimes at midnight,
Master Shallow.   232

Shal. That we have, that we have, that we
have; in faith, Sir John, we have. Our watch-
word was, 'Hem boys!' Come, let's to dinner;
come, let's to dinner. Jesus, the days that we 236
have seen! Come, come.

       Exeunt [Falstaff, Shallow, and Silence].

Bull. Good Master Corporate Bardolph, stand
my friend, and here's four Harry ten shillings in
French crowns for you. In very truth, sir, I had 240
as lief be hanged, sir, as go: and yet, for mine
own part, sir, I do not care; but rather, because
I am unwilling, and, for mine own part, have a
desire to stay with my friends: else, sir, I did 244
not care, for mine own part, so much.

Bard. Go to; stand aside.

Moul. And, good Master corporal captain, for
my old dame's sake, stand my friend: she has 248
nobody to do anything about her, when I am
gone; and she is old, and cannot help herself.
You shall have forty, sir.

Bard. Go to; stand aside.   252

Fee. By my troth, I care not; a man can die
but once; we owe God a death. I'll ne'er bear
a base mind: an 't be my destiny, so; an 't be
not, so. No man's too good to serve's prince; 256

238 Corporate: *blunder for 'Corporal'*
239 Harry ten shillings; *cf. n.*

and let it go which way it will, he that dies this
year is quit for the next.

Bard. Well said; thou'rt a good fellow.

Fee. Faith, I'll bear no base mind.   260

    Enter Falstaff and the Justices.

Fal. Come, sir, which men shall I have?

Shal. Four, of which you please.

Bard. [*To Falstaff.*] Sir, a word with you.
I have three pound to free Mouldy and Bullcalf. 264

Fal. [*Aside to Bardolph.*] Go to; well.

Shal. Come, Sir John, which four will you
have?

Fal. Do you choose for me.   268

Shal. Marry, then, Mouldy, Bullcalf, Feeble,
and Shadow.

Fal. Mouldy, and Bullcalf: for you, Mouldy,
stay at home till you are past service: and for 272
your part, Bullcalf, grow till you come unto it:
I will none of you.

Shal. Sir John, Sir John, do not yourself
wrong: they are your likeliest men, and I would 276
have you served with the best.

Fal. Will you tell me, Master Shallow, how
to choose a man? Care I for the limb, the thewes,
the stature, bulk, and big assemblance of a man! 280
Give me the spirit, Master Shallow. Here's
Wart; you see what a ragged appearance it is:
a' shall charge you and discharge you with the
motion of a pewterer's hammer, come off and on 284
swifter than he that gibbets on the brewer's
bucket. And this same half-faced fellow, Shadow,
give me this man: he presents no mark to the

enemy; the foeman may with as great aim level 288
at the edge of a penknife. And, for a retreat;
how swiftly will this Feeble the woman's tailor
run off! O! give me the spare men, and spare
me the great ones. Put me a caliver into Wart's 292
hand, Bardolph.

Bard. Hold, Wart, traverse; thus, thus, thus.

Fal. Come, manage me your caliver. So:
very well: go to: very good: exceeding good. 296
O, give me always a little, lean, old, chopp'd,
bald shot. Well said, i' faith, Wart; thou'rt a
good scab: hold, there's a tester for thee.

Shal. He is not his craft's master, he doth 300
not do it right. I remember at Mile-end Green,
when I lay at Clement's Inn,—I was then Sir
Dagonet in Arthur's show,—there was a little
quiver fellow, and a' would manage you his 304
piece thus: and a' would about and about, and
come you in, and come you in; 'rah, tah, tah,'
would a' say; 'bounce,' would a' say; and away
again would a' go, and again would a' come: I 308
shall never see such a fellow.

Fal. These fellows will do well, Master Shallow. God keep you, Master Silence: I will not
use many words with you. Fare you well, gentle- 312
men both: I thank you: I must a dozen mile
to-night. Bardolph, give the soldiers coats.

Shal. Sir John, the Lord bless you! God pros-
per your affairs! God send us peace! At your 316
return visit our house; let our old acquaintance
be renewed: peradventure I will with ye to the
court.

292 caliver: *light musket*   294 traverse: *march*
297 chopp'd: *chapped*   299 tester: *sixpence*
301-303 *Cf. n.*   304 quiver: *nimble*
306 come you in: *make a home thrust*   307 bounce: *bang*

Fal. 'Fore God I would you would, Master 320
Shallow.

Shal. Go to; I have spoke at a word.   God
keep you.

Fal. Fare you well, gentle gentlemen.   324
          Exit [*Shallow, with Silence*].
On, Bardolph; lead the men away.
          [*Exit Bardolph, with recruits.*]
As I return, I will fetch off these justices:
I do see the bottom of Justice Shallow. Lord,
Lord! how subject we old men are to this 328
vice of lying.   This same starved justice hath
done nothing but prate to me of the wildness of
his youth and the feats he hath done about
Turnbull Street; and every third word a lie, duer 332
paid to the hearer than the Turk's tribute.   I do
remember him at Clement's Inn like a man made
after supper of a cheese-paring: when a' was
naked he was for all the world like a forked 336
radish, with a head fantastically carved upon it
with a knife: a' was so forlorn that his dimen-
sions to any thick sight were invisible: a' was
the very genius of famine; yet lecherous as a 340
monkey, and the whores called him mandrake:
a' came ever in the rearward of the fashion and
sung those tunes to the over-scutched huswives
that he heard the carmen whistle, and sware 344
they were his fancies or his good-nights.   And
now is this Vice's dagger become a squire, and
talks as familiarly of John a Gaunt as if he had

322 at a word: *briefly but sincerely*
326 fetch off: *get the better of, 'take in'*   332 duer: *more duly*
343 over-scutched huswives: *cant term for 'harlots'*
344 carmen: *teamsters*
345 fancies . . . good-nights: *common names for little poems*
346 Vice's dagger: *cf. n.*

been sworn brother to him; and I'll be sworn a' 348
never saw him but once in the Tilt-yard, and
then he burst his head for crowding among the
marshal's men. I saw it and told John a Gaunt
he beat his own name; for you might have thrust 352
him and all his apparel into an eel-skin; the
case of a treble hautboy was a mansion for him,
a court; and now has he land and beefs. Well,
I'll be acquainted with him, if I return; and 356
it shall go hard but I'll make him a philosopher's two stones to me. If the young dace be a
bait for the old pike, I see no reason in the law
of nature but I may snap at him. Let time 360
shape, and there an end. *Exit.*

ACT FOURTH

Scene One

*Enter the Archbishop, Mowbray, [Lord] Bardolph,
Hastings, within the Forest of Gaultree.*

Arch. What is this forest call'd?
Hast. 'Tis Gaultree Forest, an 't shall please your
    Grace.
Arch. Here stand, my lords, and send discoverers
    forth,
To know the numbers of our enemies. 4
Hast. We have sent forth already.
Arch.   'Tis well done.
My friends and brethren in these great affairs,
I must acquaint you that I have receiv'd
New-dated letters from Northumberland; 8

354 hautboy: *slender reed instrument, oboe*
357 philosopher's two stones; *cf. n.*

Their cold intent, tenour and substance, thus:
Here doth he wish his person, with such powers
As might hold sortance with his quality;
The which he could not levy; whereupon   12
He is retir'd, to ripe his growing fortunes,
To Scotland; and concludes in hearty prayers
That your attempts may overlive the hazard
And fearful meeting of their opposite.   16
   Mowb. Thus do the hopes we have in him touch
      ground
And dash themselves to pieces.

Enter a Messenger.

   Hast.   Now, what news?
   Mess. West of this forest, scarcely off a mile,
In goodly form comes on the enemy;   20
And, by the ground they hide, I judge their number
Upon or near the rate of thirty thousand.
   Mowb. The just proportion that we gave them out.
Let us sway on and face them in the field.   24

Enter Westmoreland.

   Arch. What well-appointed leader fronts us here?
   Mowb. I think it is my Lord of Westmoreland.
   West. Health and fair greeting from our general,
The Prince, Lord John and Duke of Lancaster.   28
   Arch. Say on, my Lord of Westmoreland, in peace,
What doth concern your coming.
   West.   Then, my lord,
Unto your Grace do I in chief address
The substance of my speech. If that rebellion   32
Came like itself, in base and abject routs,

---

11 hold sortance: *be in accord*   quality: *rank*
20 form: *formation*
23 just proportion: *exact size*   gave them out: *described them*
33 routs: *gangs*

Led on by bloody youth, guarded with rags,
And countenanc'd by boys and beggary;
I say, if damn'd commotion so appear'd,   36
In his true, native, and most proper shape,
You, reverend father, and these noble lords
Had not been here, to dress the ugly form
Of base and bloody insurrection   40
With your fair honours. You, lord archbishop,
Whose see is by a civil peace maintain'd,
Whose beard the silver hand of peace hath touch'd,
Whose learning and good letters peace hath tutor'd, 44
Whose white investments figure innocence,
The dove and very blessed spirit of peace,
Wherefore do you so ill translate yourself
Out of the speech of peace that bears such grace   48
Into the harsh and boisterous tongue of war;
Turning your books to greaves, your ink to blood,
Your pens to lances, and your tongue divine
To a loud trumpet and a point of war?   52
   Arch. Wherefore do I this? so the question stands.
Briefly to this end: we are all diseas'd;
And, with our surfeiting and wanton hours
Have brought ourselves into a burning fever,   56
And we must bleed for it: of which disease
Our late king, Richard, being infected, died.
But, my most noble Lord of Westmoreland,
I take not on me here as a physician,   60
Nor do I as an enemy to peace
Troop in the throngs of military men;
But rather show a while like fearful war,
To diet rank minds sick of happiness   64
And purge the obstructions which begin to stop
Our very veins of life.   Hear me more plainly:

34 guarded: *decked*   52 point: *trumpet signal*

I have in equal balance justly weigh'd
What wrongs our arms may do, what wrongs we
    suffer,   68
And find our griefs heavier than our offences.
We see which way the stream of time doth run
And are enforc'd from our most quiet sphere
By the rough torrent of occasion;   72
And have the summary of all our griefs,
When time shall serve, to show in articles,
Which long ere this we offer'd to the king,
And might by no suit gain our audience.   76
When we are wrong'd and would unfold our griefs,
We are denied access unto his person
Even by those men that most have done us wrong.
The dangers of the days but newly gone,—   80
Whose memory is written on the earth
With yet appearing blood,—and the examples
Of every minute's instance, present now,
Have put us in these ill-beseeming arms;   84
Not to break peace, or any branch of it,
But to establish here a peace indeed,
Concurring both in name and quality.

    West. When ever yet was your appeal denied? 88
Wherein have you been galled by the king?
What peer hath been suborn'd to grate on you,
That you should seal this lawless bloody book
Of forg'd rebellion with a seal divine,   92
And consecrate commotion's bitter edge?

    Arch. My brother general, the commonwealth,
To brother born an household cruelty,
I make my quarrel in particular.   96

    West. There is no need of any such redress;
Or if there were, it not belongs to you.

69 griefs: *grievances*   93 commotion's: *insurrection's*
94-96 *Cf. n.*

Mowb. Why not to him in part, and to us all
That feel the bruises of the days before,   100
And suffer the condition of these times
To lay a heavy and unequal hand
Upon our honours?

West.   O! my good Lord Mowbray,
Construe the times to their necessities,   104
And you shall say indeed, it is the time,
And not the king, that doth you injuries.
Yet, for your part, it not appears to me
Either from the king or in the present time   108
That you should have an inch of any ground
To build a grief on: were you not restor'd
To all the Duke of Norfolk's signories,
Your noble and right well-remember'd father's?   112

Mowb. What thing, in honour, had my father lost,
That need to be reviv'd and breath'd in me?
The king that lov'd him as the state stood then,
Was force perforce compell'd to banish him: 116
And then that Harry Bolingbroke and he,
Being mounted and both roused in their seats,
Their neighing coursers daring of the spur,
Their armed staves in charge, their beavers down, 120
Their eyes of fire sparkling through sights of steel,
And the loud trumpet blowing them together,
Then, then when there was nothing could have stay'd
My father from the breast of Bolingbroke,   124
O! when the king did throw his warder down,
His own life hung upon the staff he threw;
Then threw he down himself and all their lives
That by indictment and by dint of sword   128

---

104 to: *according to*   114 breath'd: *given breath of life*
117 ff. *Cf. n.*
120 armed staves: *lances*   in charge: *in rest for the charge*
    beavers: *movable fronts of the helmets*
121 sights: *eyeholes of the helmet*   125 warder: *staff of command*

Have since miscarried under Bolingbroke.

   West. You speak, Lord Mowbray, now you know
    not what.

The Earl of Hereford was reputed then
In England the most valiant gentleman: 132
Who knows on whom Fortune would then have
    smil'd?
But if your father had been victor there,
He ne'er had borne it out of Coventry;
For all the country in a general voice   136
Cried hate upon him; and all their prayers and love
Were set on Hereford, whom they doted on
And bless'd and grac'd indeed, more than the king.
But this is mere digression from my purpose.   140
Here come I from our princely general
To know your griefs; to tell you from his Grace
That he will give you audience; and wherein
It shall appear that your demands are just,   144
You shall enjoy them; everything set off
That might so much as think you enemies.

   Mowb. But he hath forc'd us to compel this offer,
And it proceeds from policy, not love.   148

   West. Mowbray, you overween to take it so.
This offer comes from mercy, not from fear:
For, lo! within a ken our army lies
Upon mine honour, all too confident   152
To give admittance to a thought of fear.
Our battle is more full of names than yours,
Our men more perfect in the use of arms,
Our armour all as strong, our cause the best;   156
Then reason will our hearts should be as good:

129 miscarried: *perished*
131 Earl of Hereford: *King Henry, actually Duke of Hereford at
   the time of his banishment (cf. Richard II, I. iii. 21)*
145 set off: *ignored*   149 overween: *are arrogant*
151 within a ken: *within seeing distance*
154 names: *noble and soldierly names*

Say you not then our offer is compell'd.

   Mowb. Well, by my will we shall admit no parley.

   West. That argues but the shame of your
     offence: 160

A rotten case abides no handling.

   Hast. Hath the Prince John a full commission,

In very ample virtue of his father,

To hear and absolutely to determine   164

Of what conditions we shall stand upon?

   West. That is intended in the general's name.

I muse you make so slight a question.

   Arch. Then take, my Lord of Westmoreland, this
     schedule,   168

For this contains our general grievances:

Each several article herein redress'd;

All members of our cause, both here and hence,

That are insinew'd to this action,   172

Acquitted by a true substantial form;

And present execution of our wills

To us and to our purposes consign'd;

We come within our awful banks again   176

And knit our powers to the arm of peace.

   West. This will I show the general. Please you,
     lords,

In sight of both our battles we may meet;

And either end in peace, which God so frame!   180

Or to the place of difference call the swords

Which must decide it.

   Arch.   My lord, we will do so.

                          Exit Westmoreland.

   Mowb. There is a thing within my bosom tells me

That no conditions of our peace can stand.   184

163 In . . . virtue: *by complete authority*   166 intended: *implied*
167 muse: *wonder*   slight: *trivial*
172 insinew'd: *joined as by sinews*   175 consign'd; *cf. n.*
176 awful: *respectful, reverential*

Hast. Fear you not that: if we can make our
    peace
Upon such large terms, and so absolute
As our conditions shall consist upon,
Our peace shall stand as firm as rocky mountains. 188
    Mowb. Yea, but our valuation shall be such
That every slight and false-derived cause,
Yea, every idle, nice, and wanton reason
Shall to the king taste of this action;   192
That, were our royal faiths martyrs in love,
We shall be winnow'd with so rough a wind
That even our corn shall seem as light as chaff
And good from bad find no partition.   196
    Arch. No, no, my lord. Note this; the king is
    weary
Of dainty and such picking grievances:
For he hath found to end one doubt by death
Revives two greater in the heirs of life;   200
And therefore will he wipe his tables clean,
And keep no tell-tale to his memory
That may repeat and history his loss
To new remembrance; for full well he knows   204
He cannot so precisely weed this land
As his misdoubts present occasion:
His foes are so enrooted with his friends
That, plucking to unfix an enemy,   208
He doth unfasten so and shake a friend.
So that this land, like an offensive wife,
That hath enrag'd him on to offer strokes,
As he is striking, holds his infant up   212
And hangs resolv'd correction in the arm
That was uprear'd to execution.

189 our valuation: *the king's estimation of us*   191 nice: *trivial*
198 picking: *fastidious*   206 misdoubts: *suspicions*
213 hangs: *suspends*
    resolv'd correction: *chastisement which had been determined upon*

Hast. Besides, the king hath wasted all his rods
On late offenders, that he now doth lack   216
The very instruments of chastisement;
So that his power, like to a fangless lion,
May offer, but not hold.
    Arch.   'Tis very true:
And therefore be assur'd, my good lord marshal,   220
If we do now make our atonement well,
Our peace will, like a broken limb united,
Grow stronger for the breaking.
    Mowb.   Be it so.
Here is return'd my Lord of Westmoreland.   224

Enter Westmoreland.

West. The prince is here at hand: pleaseth your
    lordship,
To meet his Grace just distance 'tween our armies?
    Mowb. Your Grace of York, in God's name then,
    set forward.
    Arch. Before, and greet his Grace: my lord, we
    come.   228

Scene Two

[The Same]

Enter Prince John of Lancaster and his army.

Lanc. You are well encounter'd here, my cousin
    Mowbray:
Good day to you, gentle lord archbishop;
And so to you, Lord Hastings, and to all.
My Lord of York, it better show'd with you.   4
When that your flock, assembled by the bell,

219 offer: *attack*   221 atonement: *reconciliation*
228 Before: *go before me*   Scene Two; *cf. n.*

Encircled you to hear with reverence
Your exposition on the holy text
Than now to see you here an iron man,   8
Cheering a rout of rebels with your drum,
Turning the word to sword and life to death.
That man that sits within a monarch's heart
And ripens in the sunshine of his favour,   12
Would he abuse the countenance of the king,
Alack! what mischiefs might he set abroach
In shadow of such greatness. With you, lord bishop,
It is even so. Who hath not heard it spoken   16
How deep you were within the books of God?
To us the speaker in his parliament;
To us the imagin'd voice of God himself;
The very opener and intelligencer   20
Between the grace, the sanctities of heaven,
And our dull workings. O! who shall believe
But you misuse the reverence of your place,
Employ the countenance and grace of heaven,   24
As a false favourite doth his prince's name,
In deeds dishonourable? You have taken up,
Under the counterfeited zeal of God,
The subjects of his substitute, my father;   28
And both against the peace of heaven and him
Have here upswarm'd them.
   Arch.   Good my Lord of Lancaster,
I am not here against your father's peace;
But, as I told my Lord of Westmoreland,   32
The time misorder'd doth, in common sense,
Crowd us and crush us to this monstrous form,
To hold our safety up. I sent your Grace
The parcels and particulars of our grief,—   36

20 intelligencer: *interpreter*   22 workings: *actions*
26 taken up: *levied*

The which hath been with scorn shov'd from the
    court,—
Whereon this Hydra son of war is born;
Whose dangerous eyes may well be charm'd asleep
With grant of our most just and right desires,   40
And true obedience, of this madness cur'd,
Stoop tamely to the foot of majesty.
    Mowb. If not, we ready are to try our fortunes
To the last man.
    Hast.   And though we here fall down, 44
We have supplies to second our attempt:
If they miscarry, theirs shall second them;
And so success of mischief shall be born,
And heir from heir shall hold this quarrel up   48
Whiles England shall have generation.
    Lanc. You are too shallow, Hastings, much too
    shallow,
To sound the bottom of the after-times.
    West. Pleaseth your Grace, to answer them
    directly   52
How far forth you do like their articles.
    Lanc. I like them all, and do allow them well;
And swear here, by the honour of my blood,
My father's purposes have been mistook,   56
And some about him have too lavishly
Wrested his meaning and authority.
My lord, these griefs shall be with speed redress'd;
Upon my soul, they shall. If this may please you, 60
Discharge your powers unto their several counties,
As we will ours: and here between the armies
Let's drink together friendly and embrace,
That all their eyes may bear those tokens home   64
Of our restored love and amity.

47 success: *succession*

Arch. I take your princely word for these re-
dresses.

Lanc. I give it you, and will maintain my word:
And thereupon I drink unto your Grace.   68

Hast. [*To an Officer.*] Go, captain, and deliver to
the army
This news of peace: let them have pay, and part:
I know it will well please them: hie thee, captain.

                                    Exit [*Officer*].

Arch. To you, my noble Lord of Westmoreland. 72

West. I pledge your Grace: and, if you knew what
pains
I have bestow'd to breed this present peace,
You would drink freely; but my love to you
Shall show itself more openly hereafter.   76

Arch. I do not doubt you.

West.   I am glad of it.
Health to my lord and gentle cousin, Mowbray.

Mowb. You wish me health in very happy season;
For I am, on the sudden, something ill.   80

Arch. Against ill chances men are ever merry,
But heaviness foreruns the good event.

West. Therefore be merry, coz; since sudden sorrow
Serves to say thus, Some good thing comes to-morrow.   84

Arch. Believe me, I am passing light in spirit.

Mowb. So much the worse if your own rule be
true.   *Shout* [*within*].

Lanc. The word of peace is render'd: hark, how
they shout!

Mowb. This had been cheerful, after victory.   88

70 part: *depart*   81 Against: *when about to face*
82 heaviness: *depression*   85 passing: *exceedingly*
87 render'd: *reported*

Arch. A peace is of the nature of a conquest;
For then both parties nobly are subdu'd,
And neither party loser.
    Lanc.   Go, my lord,
And let our army be discharged too.   92
                            Exit [*Westmoreland*].
And, good my lord, so please you, let our trains
March by us, that we may peruse the men
We should have cop'd withal.
    Arch. Go, good Lord Hastings,   96
And, ere they be dismiss'd, let them march by.
                            Exit [*Hastings*].
    Lanc. I trust, lords, we shall lie to-night together.

                Enter Westmoreland.

Now, cousin, wherefore stands our army still?
    West. The leaders, having charge from you to
        stand,   100
Will not go off until they hear you speak.
    Lanc. They know their duties.

                Enter Hastings.

    Hast. My lord, our army is dispers'd already:
Like youthful steers unyok'd, they take their
        courses   104
East, west, north, south; or, like a school broke up,
Each hurries toward his home and sporting-place.
    West. Good tidings, my Lord Hastings; for the
        which
I do arrest thee, traitor, of high treason: 108
And you, lord archbishop, and you, Lord Mowbray,
Of capital treason I attach you both.
    Mowb. Is this proceeding just and honourable?
    West. Is your assembly so?   112

94 peruse: *inspect*

Arch. Will you thus break your faith?
Lanc.   I pawn'd thee none.
I promis'd you redress of these same grievances
Whereof you did complain; which, by mine honour,
I will perform with a most Christian care.   116
But for you, rebels, look to taste the due
Meet for rebellion and such acts as yours.
Most shallowly did you these arms commence,
Fondly brought here and foolishly sent hence.   120
Strike up our drums! pursue the scatter'd stray:
God, and not we, hath safely fought to-day.
Some guard these traitors to the block of death;
Treason's true bed, and yielder up of breath.   124
                                        Exeunt.

Scene Three

[*Another Part of the Forest*]

Alarums.   Excursions.   Enter Falstaff and Colevile.

    Fal. What's your name, sir? of what con-
dition are you, and of what place, I pray?
    Cole. I am a knight, sir; and my name is
Colevile of the dale.   4
    Fal. Well then, Colevile is your name, a
knight is your degree, and your place the dale:
Colevile shall be still your name, a traitor your
degree, and the dungeon your place, a place 8
deep enough; so shall you be still Colevile of
the dale.
    Cole. Are not you Sir John Falstaff?
    Fal. As good a man as he, sir, whoe'er I am. 12
Do ye yield, sir, or shall I sweat for you?   If

113 pawn'd: *pledged*
120 Fondly: *foolishly*

119 shallowly: *thoughtlessly*
1 condition: *rank*

I do sweat, they are the drops of thy lovers,
and they weep for thy death: therefore rouse
up fear and trembling, and do observance to 16
my mercy.

Cole. I think you are Sir John Falstaff, and
in that thought yield me.

Fal. I have a whole school of tongues in this 20
belly of mine, and not a tongue of them all
speaks any other word but my name. An I had
but a belly of any indifferency, I were simply the
most active fellow in Europe: my womb, my 24
womb, my womb undoes me. Here comes our
general.

Enter Prince John, Westmoreland and the rest.

Lanc. The heat is past, follow no further now.
Call in the powers, good cousin Westmoreland.   28
                                    [*Exit Westmoreland.*]
Now, Falstaff, where have you been all this while?
When everything is ended, then you come:
These tardy tricks of yours will, on my life,
One time or other break some gallows' back.   32

Fal. I would be sorry, my lord, but it should
be thus: I never knew yet but rebuke and check
was the reward of valour. Do you think me a
swallow, an arrow, or a bullet? have I, in my 36
poor and old motion, the expedition of thought?
I have speeded hither with the very extremest
inch of possibility; I have foundered nine score
and odd posts; and here, travel-tainted as I am, 40
have, in my pure and immaculate valour, taken
Sir John Colevile of the dale, a most furious

16 observance: *homage*   23 indifferency: *moderate size*
27 heat: *race, pursuit*   34 check: *reproof*
37 expedition: *speed*   40 posts: *post-horses*

knight and valorous enemy. But what of that?
he saw me, and yielded; that I may justly say 44
with the hook-nosed fellow of Rome, 'I came,
saw, and overcame.'

Lanc. It was more of his courtesy than your
deserving.   48

Fal. I know not: here he is, and here I yield
him; and I beseech your Grace, let it be booked
with the rest of this day's deeds; or, by the Lord,
I will have it in a particular ballad else, with 52
mine own picture on the top on 't, Colevile
kissing my foot. To the which course if I be
enforced, if you do not all show like gilt two-
pences to me, and I in the clear sky of fame 56
o'ershine you as much as the full moon doth
the cinders of the element, which show like pins'
heads to her, believe not the word of the noble.
Therefore let me have right, and let desert 60
mount.

Lanc. Thine's too heavy to mount.

Fal. Let it shine then.

Lanc. Thine's too thick to shine.   64

Fal. Let it do something, my good lord, that
may do me good, and call it what you will.

Lanc. Is thy name Colevile?

Cole. It is, my lord.   68

Lanc. A famous rebel art thou, Colevile.

Fal. And a famous true subject took him.

Cole. I am, my lord, but as my betters are
That led me hither: had they been rul'd by me 72
You should have won them dearer than you have.

Fal. I know not how they sold themselves:

58 cinders: *glowing coals, stars*   element: *sky*

but thou, like a kind fellow, gavest thyself away
gratis, and I thank thee for thee.   76

Enter Westmoreland.

Lanc. Now, have you left pursuit?
West. Retreat is made and execution stay'd.
Lanc. Send Colevile with his confederates
To York, to present execution.   80
Blunt, lead him hence, and see you guard him sure.
                    Exit [Blunt] with Colevile.
And now dispatch we toward the court, my lords:
I hear, the king my father is sore sick:
Our news shall go before us to his majesty,   84
Which, cousin [*addressing Westmoreland*], you shall
        bear, to comfort him;
And we with sober speed will follow you.
    Fal. My lord, I beseech you, give me leave to go,
Through Gloucestershire, and when you come to
        court   88
Stand my good lord, pray, in your good report.
    Lanc. Fare you well, Falstaff: I, in my condition,
Shall better speak of you than you deserve.
                    [Exeunt all but Falstaff.]
    Fal. I would you had but the wit: 'twere 92
better than your dukedom. Good faith, this
same young sober-blooded boy doth not love
me; nor a man cannot make him laugh; but
that's no marvel, he drinks no wine. There's 96
never none of these demure boys come to any
proof; for thin drink doth so over-cool their
blood, and making many fish-meals, that they
fall into a kind of male green-sickness; and then, 100

80 present: *immediate*   82 dispatch we: *let us hasten*
89 Stand my good lord: *be my kind patron*
90 condition: *official capacity*
97, 98 come to any proof: *turn out well*

when they marry, they get wenches. They
are generally fools and cowards, which some of
us should be too but for inflammation. A good
sherris-sack hath a two-fold operation in it. 104
It ascends me into the brain; dries me there all
the foolish and dull and crudy vapours which
environ it; makes it apprehensive, quick, forgetive, full of nimble, fiery and delectable shapes; 108
which, deliver'd o'er to the voice, the tongue,
which is the birth, becomes excellent wit. The
second property of your excellent sherris is, the
warming of the blood; which, before cold and 112
settled, left the liver white and pale, which is
the badge of pusillanimity and cowardice: but
the sherris warms it and makes it course from
the inwards to the parts extreme. It illumineth 116
the face, which, as a beacon, gives warning to
all the rest of this little kingdom, man, to arm;
and then the vital commoners and inland petty
spirits muster me all to their captain, the heart, 120
who, great and puffed up with this retinue, doth
any deed of courage; and this valour comes of
sherris. So that skill in the weapon is nothing
without sack, for that sets it a-work; and learn- 124
ing, a mere hoard of gold kept by a devil till
sack commences it and sets it in act and use.
Hereof comes it that Prince Harry is valiant;
for the cold blood he did naturally inherit of 128
his father, he hath, like lean, sterile, and bare
land, manured, husbanded, and tilled, with excellent endeavour of drinking good and good
store of fertile sherris, that he is become very 132
hot and valiant. If I had a thousand sons, the

101 get wenches: *beget girls*   104 sherris-sack: *sherry*
106 crudy: *crude, raw*   107 forgetive: *inventive*   125 *Cf. n.*

first human principle I would teach them should
be, to forswear thin potations and to addict
themselves to sack.   136

Enter Bardolph.

How now, Bardolph?
    Bard. The army is discharged all and gone.
    Fal. Let them go. I'll through Gloucester-
shire; and there will I visit Master Robert 140
Shallow, esquire: I have him already tempering
between my finger and my thumb, and shortly
will I seal with him. Come away.   *Exeunt.*

Scene Four

[*Westminster. The Jerusalem Chamber*]

*Enter the King, Warwick, Thomas Duke of Clarence,
Humphrey of Gloucester [and others].*

    King. Now, lords, if God doth give successful end
To this debate that bleedeth at our doors,
We will our youth lead on to higher fields
And draw no swords, but what are sanctified.   4
Our navy is address'd, our power collected,
Our substitutes in absence well invested,
And everything lies level to our wish:
Only, we want a little personal strength;   8
And pause us, till these rebels, now afoot,
Come underneath the yoke of government.
    War. Both which we doubt not but your majesty
Shall soon enjoy.
    King.   Humphrey, my son of Gloucester, 12

141-143 tempering . . . seal: *the allusion is to sealing-wax*
Scene Four S. d. Jerusalem Chamber; *cf. n.*
5 address'd: *prepared*   6 invested: *invested with authority*

Where is the prince your brother?

  Glo. I think he's gone to hunt, my lord, at Windsor.

  King. And how accompanied?

  Glo.   I do not know, my lord.

  King. Is not his brother Thomas of Clarence with
    him?   16

  Glo. No, my good lord; he is in presence here.

  Cla. What would my lord and father?

  King. Nothing but well to thee, Thomas of
    Clarence.

How chance thou art not with the prince thy
    brother?   20

He loves thee, and thou dost neglect him, Thomas;

Thou hast a better place in his affection

Than all thy brothers: cherish it, my boy,

And noble offices thou mayst effect   24

Of mediation, after I am dead,

Between his greatness and thy other brethren:

Therefore omit him not; blunt not his love,

Nor lose the good advantage of his grace   28

By seeming cold or careless of his will;

For he is gracious, if he be observ'd:

He hath a tear for pity and a hand

Open as day for melting charity;   32

Yet, notwithstanding, being incens'd, he's flint;

As humorous as winter, and as sudden

As flaws congealed in the spring of day.

His temper therefore must be well observ'd: 36

Chide him for faults, and do it reverently,

When you perceive his blood inclin'd to mirth;

But, being moody, give him line and scope,

Till that his passions, like a whale on ground, 40

27 omit: *neglect*   30 observ'd: *humored*
33-35 *Cf. n.*

Confound themselves with working.   Learn this,
    Thomas,
And thou shalt prove a shelter to thy friends,
A hoop of gold to bind thy brothers in,
That the united vessel of their blood,   44
Mingled with venom of suggestion—
As, force perforce, the age will pour it in—
Shall never leak, though it do work as strong
As aconitum or rash gunpowder.   48
    Cla. I shall observe him with all care and love.
    King. Why art thou not at Windsor with him,
      Thomas?
    Cla. He is not there to-day; he dines in London.
    King. And how accompanied? canst thou tell
      that?   52
    Cla. With Poins and other his continual followers.
    King. Most subject is the fattest soil to weeds;
And he, the noble image of my youth,
Is overspread with them: therefore my grief   56
Stretches itself beyond the hour of death:
The blood weeps from my heart when I do shape
In forms imaginary the unguided days
And rotten times that you shall look upon   60
When I am sleeping with my ancestors.
For when his headstrong riot hath no curb,
When rage and hot blood are his counsellors,
When means and lavish manners meet together,   64
O! with what wings shall his affections fly
Towards fronting peril and oppos'd decay.
    War. My gracious lord, you look beyond him quite:
The prince but studies his companions   68
Like a strange tongue, wherein, to gain the language,
'Tis needful that the most immodest word

41 Confound: *exhaust*
65 affections: *inclinations*
44-48 *Cf. n.*
67 look beyond: *misjudge*

Be look'd upon, and learn'd; which once attain'd,
Your highness knows, comes to no further use   72
But to be known and hated. So, like gross terms,
The prince will in the perfectness of time
Cast off his followers; and their memory
Shall as a pattern or a measure live,   76
By which his Grace must mete the lives of others,
Turning past evils to advantages.
  King. 'Tis seldom when the bee doth leave her
    comb
In the dead carrion.

Enter Westmoreland.

              Who's here? Westmoreland! 80
  West. Health to my sovereign, and new happiness
Added to that that I am to deliver!
Prince John your son doth kiss your Grace's hand:
Mowbray, the Bishop Scroop, Hastings and all   84
Are brought to the correction of your law.
There is not now a rebel's sword unsheath'd,
But Peace puts forth her olive everywhere.
The manner how this action hath been borne   88
Here at more leisure may your highness read,
With every course in his particular.
  King. O Westmoreland! thou art a summer bird,
Which ever in the haunch of winter sings   92
The lifting up of day.

Enter Harcourt.

             Look! here's more news.
  Har. From enemies heaven keep your majesty;
And, when they stand against you, may they fall
As those that I am come to tell you of!   96

The Earl Northumberland, and the Lord Bardolph,
With a great power of English and of Scots,
Are by the sheriff of Yorkshire overthrown.
The manner and true order of the fight   100
This packet, please it you, contains at large.

    King. And wherefore should these good news make
       me sick?
Will Fortune never come with both hands full
But write her fair words still in foulest letters?   104
She either gives a stomach and no food;
Such are the poor, in health; or else a feast
And takes away the stomach; such are the rich,
That have abundance and enjoy it not.   108
I should rejoice now at this happy news,
And now my sight fails, and my brain is giddy.
O me! come near me, now I am much ill.

    Glo. Comfort, your majesty!

    Cla.   O my royal father!   112

    West. My sovereign lord, cheer up yourself: look
       up!

    War. Be patient, princes: you do know these fits
Are with his highness very ordinary:
Stand from him, give him air; he'll straight be
    well.   116

    Cla. No, no; he cannot long hold out these pangs:
The incessant care and labour of his mind
Hath wrought the mure that should confine it in
So thin, that life looks through and will break out.   120

    Glo. The people fear me; for they do observe
Unfather'd heirs and loathly births of nature:
The seasons change their manners, as the year

105 stomach: *appetite*   119 wrought the mure: *worn the wall*
121 fear: *frighten*
122 (*Such portents as*) *creatures born without parents and other
    monstrosities*   123 as: *as if*

Had found some months asleep and leap'd them
    over.   124
   Cla. The river hath thrice flow'd, no ebb between;
And the old folk, time's doting chronicles,
Say it did so a little time before
That our great-grandsire, Edward, sick'd and died. 128
   War. Speak lower, princes, for the king recovers.
   Glo. This apoplexy will certain be his end.
   King. I pray you take me up, and bear me hence
Into some other chamber: softly, pray.   132
    [*Attendants and Lords take the King up, convey
      him into an inner room, and lay him upon
      a bed.*]

Scene Five

[*Another Chamber*

*King Henry lying on a bed: Clarence, Gloucester,
   Warwick, and Others in attendance.*]

   King. Let there be no noise made, my gentle
    friends;
Unless some dull and favourable hand
Will whisper music to my weary spirit.
   War. Call for the music in the other room.   4
   King. Set me the crown upon my pillow here.
   Cla. His eye is hollow, and he changes much.
   War. Less noise, less noise!

Enter Prince Henry.

   Prince.   Who saw the Duke of Clarence?
   Cla. I am here, brother, full of heaviness.   8
   Prince. How now! rain within doors, and none
    abroad!

2 *dull: soothing, drowsy*

How doth the king?

    Glo.   Exceeding ill.

    Prince.   Heard he the good news yet

Tell it him.

    Glo. He alter'd much upon the hearing it.   1

    Prince. If he be sick with joy, he'll recover without physic.

    War. Not so much noise, my lords. Sweet prince speak low;

The king your father is dispos'd to sleep.   1

    Cla. Let us withdraw into the other room.

    War. Will 't please your Grace to go along with us?

    Prince. No; I will sit and watch here by the king.

                [Exeunt all but the Prince.

Why doth the crown lie there upon his pillow,   2

Being so troublesome a bedfellow?

O polish'd perturbation! golden care!

That keep'st the ports of slumber open wide

To many a watchful night! Sleep with it now!   2

Yet not so sound, and half so deeply sweet

As he whose brow with homely biggin bound

Snores out the watch of night. O majesty!

When thou dost pinch thy bearer, thou dost sit   2

Like a rich armour worn in heat of day,

That scalds with safety. By his gates of breath

There lies a downy feather which stirs not:

Did he suspire, that light and weightless down   3

Perforce must move. My gracious lord! my father

This sleep is sound indeed; this is a sleep

That from this golden rigol hath divorc'd

So many English kings. Thy due from me   3

23 ports: *gates*   26 biggin: *nightcap*
30 with safety: *while it gives safety*   32 suspire: *breathe*
35 rigol: *circle, crown*

s tears and heavy sorrows of the blood,
Which nature, love, and filial tenderness
Shall, O dear father! pay thee plenteously:
My due from thee is this imperial crown,   40
Which, as immediate from thy place and blood,
Derives itself to me. Lo! here it sits,

                    [*Putting it on his head.*]

Which God shall guard; and put the world's whole
    strength
Into one giant arm, it shall not force   44
This lineal honour from me. This from thee
Will I to mine leave, as 'tis left to me.   *Exit.*
    King. [*Waking.*] Warwick! Gloucester! Clarence!

Enter Warwick, Gloucester, Clarence [and the rest].

    Cla.   Doth the king call?
    War. What would your majesty? How fares your
        Grace?   48
    King. Why did you leave me here alone, my lords?
    Cla. We left the prince my brother here, my liege,
Who undertook to sit and watch by you.
    King. The Prince of Wales! Where is he? let me
        see him: 52
He is not here.
    War. This door is open; he is gone this way.
    Glo. He came not through the chamber where we
        stay'd.
    King. Where is the crown? who took it from my
        pillow?   56
    War. When we withdrew, my liege, we left it here.
    King. The prince hath ta'en it hence: go, seek him
        out.
Is he so hasty that he doth suppose

41 immediate: *next in line*

My sleep my death?   6(

Find him, my Lord of Warwick; chide him hither.

                                [Exit Warwick.]

This part of his conjoins with my disease,

And helps to end me. See, sons, what things you are

How quickly nature falls into revolt   64

When gold becomes her object!

For this the foolish over-careful fathers

Have broke their sleep with thoughts,

Their brains with care, their bones with industry; 68

For this they have engrossed and pil'd up

The canker'd heaps of strange-achieved gold;

For this they have been thoughtful to invest

Their sons with arts and martial exercises: 72

When, like the bee, culling from every flower

The virtuous sweets,

Our thighs packed with wax, our mouths with honey,

We bring it to the hive, and like the bees,   7(

Are murder'd for our pains. This bitter taste

Yield his engrossments to the ending father.

                 Enter Warwick.

Now, where is he that will not stay so long

Till his friend sickness hath determin'd me?   80

   War. My lord, I found the prince in the next

     room,

Washing with kindly tears his gentle cheeks,

With such a deep demeanour in great sorrow

That tyranny, which never quaff'd but blood,   84

Would, by beholding him, have wash'd his knife

With gentle eye-drops. He is coming hither.

   King. But wherefore did he take away the crown?

---

62 part: *act*   69 engrossed: *amassed*
70 canker'd: *tarnished*   strange-achieved: *gained in foreign lands*
74 virtuous: *beneficial*   80 determin'd: *ended*
82 kindly: *natural*

Enter Prince Henry.

Lo, where he comes. Come hither to me, Harry.   88
Depart the chamber, leave us here alone.
                Exeunt [Warwick, and the rest].
  Prince. I never thought to hear you speak again.
  King. Thy wish was father, Harry, to that
    thought:
I stay too long by thee, I weary thee.   92
Dost thou so hunger for mine empty chair
That thou wilt needs invest thee with my honours
Before thy hour be ripe? O foolish youth!
Thou seek'st the greatness that will overwhelm
    thee.   96
Stay but a little; for my cloud of dignity
Is held from falling with so weak a wind
That it will quickly drop: my day is dim.
Thou hast stol'n that which after some few hours   100
Were thine without offence; and at my death
Thou hast seal'd up my expectation:
Thy life did manifest thou lov'dst me not,
And thou wilt have me die assur'd of it.   104
Thou hid'st a thousand daggers in thy thoughts,
Which thou hast whetted on thy stony heart,
To stab at half an hour of my life.
What! canst thou not forbear me half an hour?   108
Then get thee gone and dig my grave thyself,
And bid the merry bells ring to thine ear
That thou art crowned, not that I am dead.
Let all the tears that should bedew my hearse   112
Be drops of balm to sanctify thy head:
Only compound me with forgotten dust;
Give that which gave thee life unto the worms.
Pluck down my officers, break my decrees;   116

102 seal'd up: *confirmed fully*

For now a time is come to mock at form.
Harry the Fifth is crown'd! Up, vanity!
Down, royal state! all you sage counsellors, hence!
And to the English court assemble now,   120
From every region, apes of idleness!
Now, neighbour confines, purge you of your scum:
Have you a ruffian that will swear, drink, dance,
Revel the night, rob, murder, and commit   124
The oldest sins the newest kind of ways?
Be happy, he will trouble you no more:
England shall double gild his treble guilt.
England shall give him office, honour, might;   128
For the fifth Harry from curb'd licence plucks
The muzzle of restraint, and the wild dog
Shall flesh his tooth in every innocent.
O my poor kingdom! sick with civil blows,   132
When that my care could not withhold thy riots,
What wilt thou do when riot is thy care?
O! thou wilt be a wilderness again,
Peopled with wolves, thy old inhabitants.   136

  Prince. O! pardon me, my liege; but for my tears,
The moist impediments unto my speech,
I had forestall'd this dear and deep rebuke
Ere you with grief had spoke and I had heard   140
The course of it so far. There is your crown;
And he that wears the crown immortally
Long guard it yours! If I affect it more
Than as your honour and as your renown,   144
Let me no more from this obedience rise,—
Which my most inward, true, and duteous spirit
Teacheth,—this prostrate and exterior bending.
God witness with me, when I here came in,   148
And found no course of breath within your majesty,

117 form: *order*   118 vanity: *folly*   134 care: *special study*
139 dear: *earnest*   143 affect: *aspire to*

How cold it struck my heart! if I do feign,
O! let me in my present wildness die
And never live to show the incredulous world   152
The noble change that I have purposed.
Coming to look on you, thinking you dead,
And dead almost, my liege, to think you were,
I spake unto the crown as having sense,   156
And thus upbraided it: 'The care on thee depending
Hath fed upon the body of my father;
Therefore, thou best of gold art worst of gold:
Other, less fine in carat, is more precious,   160
Preserving life in medicine potable:
But thou most fine, most honour'd, most renown'd,
Hast eat thy bearer up.' Thus, my most royal liege,
Accusing it, I put it on my head,   164
To try with it, as with an enemy
That had before my face murder'd my father,
The quarrel of a true inheritor.
But if it did infect my blood with joy,   168
Or swell my thoughts to any strain of pride;
If any rebel or vain spirit of mine
Did with the least affection of a welcome
Give entertainment to the might of it,   172
Let God for ever keep it from my head,
And make me as the poorest vassal is
That doth with awe and terror kneel to it!
    King. O my son!   176
God put it in thy mind to take it hence,
That thou mightst win the more thy father's love,
Pleading so wisely in excuse of it.
Come hither, Harry: sit thou by my bed;   180
And hear, I think, the very latest counsel
That ever I shall breathe. God knows, my son,

161 medicine potable; *cf. n.*

By what by-paths and indirect crook'd ways
I met this crown; and I myself know well   184
How troublesome it sat upon my head:
To thee it shall descend with better quiet,
Better opinion, better confirmation;
For all the soil of the achievement goes   188
With me into the earth. It seem'd in me
But as an honour snatch'd with boisterous hand,
And I had many living to upbraid
My gain of it by their assistances;   192
Which daily grew to quarrel and to bloodshed,
Wounding supposed peace. All these bold fears
Thou seest with peril I have answered;
For all my reign hath been but as a scene   196
Acting that argument; and now my death
Changes the mode: for what in me was purchas'd,
Falls upon thee in a more fairer sort;
So thou the garment wear'st successively.   200
Yet, though thou stand'st more sure than I could do,
Thou art not firm enough, since griefs are green;
And all my friends, which thou must make thy
        friends,
Have but their stings and teeth newly ta'en out;   204
By whose fell working I was first advanc'd,
And by whose power I well might lodge a fear
To be again displac'd: which to avoid,
I cut them off; and had a purpose now   208
To lead out many to the Holy Land,
Lest rest and lying still might make them look
Too near unto my state. Therefore, my Harry,
Be it thy course to busy giddy minds   212
With foreign quarrels; that action, hence borne out,

188 soil: *pollution*   197 argument: *story*
198 mode; *cf. n.*   purchas'd: *acquired by my own act, not inherited*
200 successively: *by right of succession*
213 hence: *in other lands*

May waste the memory of the former days.
More would I, but my lungs are wasted so
That strength of speech is utterly denied me.   216
How I came by the crown, O God, forgive!
And grant it may with thee in true peace live.
  Prince. My gracious liege,
You won it, wore it, kept it, gave it me;   220
Then plain and right must my possession be:
Which I with more than with a common pain
'Gainst all the world will rightfully maintain.
  Enter Lord John of Lancaster, and Warwick.
  King. Look, look, here comes my John of Lan-
    caster.   224
  Lanc. Health, peace, and happiness to my royal
    father!
  King. Thou bring'st me happiness and peace, son
    John;
But health, alack, with youthful wings is flown
From this bare wither'd trunk: upon thy sight   228
My worldly business makes a period.
Where is my Lord of Warwick?
  Prince.   My Lord of Warwick!
    [*Warwick comes forward.*]
  King. Doth any name particular belong
Unto the lodging where I first did swound?   232
  War. 'Tis call'd Jerusalem, my noble lord.
  King. Laud be to God! even there my life must
    end.
It hath been prophesied to me many years
I should not die but in Jerusalem,   236
Which vainly I suppos'd the Holy Land.
But bear me to that chamber; there I'll lie:
In that Jerusalem shall Harry die.   *Exeunt.*
214 waste: *consume*

ACT FIFTH

Scene One

[*Justice Shallow's House in Gloucestershire*]

Enter Shallow, Falstaff, Bardolph [and Bardolph's boy].

Shal. By cock and pie, sir, you shall not away to-night. What! Davy, I say.

Fal. You must excuse me, Master Robert Shallow. 4

Shal. I will not excuse you; you shall not be excused; excuses shall not be admitted; there is no excuse shall serve; you shall not be excused. Why, Davy! 8

Enter Davy.

Davy. Here, sir.

Shal. Davy, Davy, Davy, Davy, let me see, Davy; let me see: yea, marry, William cook, bid him come hither. Sir John, you shall not be 12 excused.

Davy. Marry, sir, thus; those precepts cannot be served: and again, sir, shall we sow the headland with wheat? 16

Shal. With red wheat, Davy. But for William cook: are there no young pigeons?

Davy. Yes, sir. Here is now the smith's note for shoeing and plough-irons. 20

Shal. Let it be cast and paid. Sir John, you shall not be excused.

Davy. Now, sir, a new link to the bucket

1 cock and pie; *cf. n.*　　　14 precepts: *summonses*
21 cast: *reckoned*

must needs be had: and, sir, do you mean to 24
stop any of William's wages, about the sack he
lost the other day at Hinckley fair?

Shal. A' shall answer it.   Some pigeons,
Davy, a couple of short-legged hens, a joint of 28
mutton, and any petty little tiny kickshaws,
tell William cook.

Davy. Doth the man of war stay all night,
sir?   32

Shal. Yea, Davy.   I will use him well.   A
friend i' the court is better than a penny in
purse.   Use his men well, Davy, for they are
arrant knaves, and will backbite.   36

Davy. No worse than they are back-bitten,
sir; for they have marvellous foul linen.

Shal. Well conceited, Davy: about thy business, Davy.   40

Davy. I beseech you, sir, to countenance
William Visor of Wincot against Clement Perkes
o' the hill.

Shal. There is many complaints, Davy, 44
against that Visor: that Visor is an arrant
knave, on my knowledge.

Davy. I grant your worship that he is a
knave, sir; but yet, God forbid, sir, but a knave 48
should have some countenance at his friend's
request.   An honest man, sir, is able to speak for
himself, when a knave is not.   I have served
your worship truly, sir, this eight years; and if 52
I cannot once or twice in a quarter bear out a
knave against an honest man, I have but a very
little credit with your worship.   The knave is

---

29 kickshaws: *fancy dishes*   39 Well conceited: *cleverly put*
41 countenance: *favor*

mine honest friend, sir; therefore, I beseech your 56
worship, let him be countenanced.

Shal. Go to; I say he shall have no wrong.
Look about, Davy. [*Exit Davy.*] Where are you,
Sir John? Come, come, come; off with your 60
boots. Give me your hand, Master Bardolph.

Bard. I am glad to see your worship.

Shal. I thank thee with all my heart, kind
Master Bardolph:—[*To the Page.*] and wel- 64
come, my tall fellow. Come, Sir John.

Fal. I'll follow you, good Master Robert
Shallow. [*Exit Shallow.*] Bardolph, look to
our horses. [*Exeunt Bardolph and Page.*] If I 68
were sawed into quantities, I should make four
dozen of such bearded hermit's staves as Master
Shallow. It is a wonderful thing to see the
semblable coherence of his men's spirits and his: 72
they, by observing him, do bear themselves like
foolish justices; he, by conversing with them, is
turned into a justice-like serving-man. Their
spirits are so married in conjunction with the 76
participation of society that they flock together
in consent, like so many wild-geese. If I had a
suit to Master Shallow, I would humour his men
with the imputation of being near their master: 80
if to his men, I would curry with Master Shallow
that no man could better command his servants.
It is certain that either wise bearing or ignorant
carriage is caught, as men take diseases, one of 84
another: therefore let men take heed of their
company. I will devise matter enough out of
this Shallow to keep Prince Harry in continual

69 quantities: *small pieces*
72 semblable coherence: *approach to likeness*
78 consent: *agreement*

laughter the wearing out of six fashions,—which 88
is four terms, or two actions,—and a' shall laugh
without intervallums.   O! it is much that a lie
with a slight oath and a jest with a sad brow
will do with a fellow that never had the ache in 92
his shoulders.   O! you shall see him laugh till
his face be like a wet cloak ill laid up!

Shal. [*Within.*] Sir John!

Fal. I come, Master Shallow: I come, Master 96
Shallow.   [*Exit.*]

Scene Two

[Westminster.   The Palace]

*Enter the Earl of Warwick and the Lord Chief
Justice.*

War. How now, my Lord Chief Justice! whither
    away?

Ch. Just. How doth the king?

War. Exceeding well: his cares are now all ended.

Ch. Just. I hope not dead.

War.   He's walk'd the way of nature; 4
And to our purposes he lives no more.

Ch. Just. I would his majesty had call'd me with
    him:
The service that I truly did his life
Hath left me open to all injuries.   8

War. Indeed I think the young king loves you not.

Ch. Just. I know he doth not, and do arm myself
To welcome the condition of the time,
Which cannot look more hideously upon me   12

89 terms: *i.e., of court*   actions: *legal actions for debt*
90 intervallums: *intervals*   91 sad: *sober*
94 ill laid up: *carelessly put away*

Than I have drawn it in my fantasy.

Enter John of Lancaster, Gloucester, Clarence
[Westmoreland, and others].

War. Here come the heavy issue of dead Harry:
O! that the living Harry had the temper
Of him, the worst of these three gentlemen.   16
How many nobles then should hold their places,
That must strike sail to spirits of vile sort!

    Ch. Just. O God! I fear all will be overturn'd.

    Lanc. Good morrow, cousin Warwick, good mor-
       row.   20

    Glo. }
           } Good morrow, cousin.
    Cla. }

    Lanc. We meet like men that had forgot to speak.

    War. We do remember; but our argument
Is all too heavy to admit much talk.   24

    Lanc. Well, peace be with him that hath made us
       heavy!

    Ch. Just. Peace be with us, lest we be heavier!

    Glo. O! good my lord, you have lost a friend
       indeed;
And I dare swear you borrow not that face   28
Of seeming sorrow; it is sure your own.

    Lanc. Though no man be assur'd what grace to
       find,
You stand in coldest expectation.
I am the sorrier; would 'twere otherwise.   32

    Cla. Well, you must now speak Sir John Falstaff
       fair,
Which swims against your stream of quality.

    Ch. Just. Sweet princes, what I did, I did in
       honour,

14 heavy: *sorrowful*   23 argument: *subject of conversation*
31 coldest: *most hopeless*   34 *Cf. n.*

Led by the impartial conduct of my soul;   36
And never shall you see that I will beg
A ragged and forestall'd remission.
If truth and upright innocency fail me,
I'll to the king my master that is dead,   40
And tell him who hath sent me after him.

  War. Here comes the prince.

                 Enter the Prince and Blunt.

  Ch. Just. Good   morrow,   and   God   save   your
     majesty!

  Prince. This new and gorgeous garment, maj-
     esty,   44
Sits not so easy on me as you think.
Brothers, you mix your sadness with some fear:
This is the English, not the Turkish court;
Not Amurath an Amurath succeeds,   48
But Harry Harry. Yet be sad, good brothers,
For, by my faith, it very well becomes you:
Sorrow so royally in you appears
That I will deeply put the fashion on   52
And wear it in my heart. Why then, be sad;
But entertain no more of it, good brothers,
Than a joint burden laid upon us all.
For me, by heaven, I bid you be assur'd,   56
I'll be your father and your brother too;
Let me but bear your love, I'll bear your cares:
Yet weep that Harry's dead, and so will I;
But Harry lives that shall convert those tears   60
By number into hours of happiness.

  Brothers. We hope no other from your majesty.

  Prince. You all look strangely on me: [*To the
     Chief Justice.*] and you most;

38 ragged: *beggarly*
   forestall'd remission: *pardon that is sure not to be granted*
48 *Cf. n.*

You are, I think, assur'd I love you not.   64

    Ch. Just. I am assur'd, if I be measur'd rightly,
Your majesty hath no just cause to hate me.

    Prince. No?

How might a prince of my great hopes forget   68
So great indignities you laid upon me?
What! rate, rebuke, and roughly send to prison
The immediate heir of England! Was this easy?
May this be wash'd in Lethe, and forgotten?   72

    Ch. Just. I then did use the person of your
        father;

The image of his power lay then in me:
And, in the administration of his law,
Whiles I was busy for the commonwealth,   76
Your highness pleased to forget my place,
The majesty and power of law and justice,
The image of the king whom I presented,
And struck me in my very seat of judgment;   80
Whereon, as an offender to your father,
I gave bold way to my authority,
And did commit you. If the deed were ill,
Be you contented, wearing now the garland,   84
To have a son set your decrees at nought,
To pluck down justice from your awful bench,
To trip the course of law, and blunt the sword
That guards the peace and safety of your person. 38
Nay, more, to spurn at your most royal image
And mock your workings in a second body.
Question your royal thoughts, make the case yours;
Be now the father and propose a son,   92
Hear your own dignity so much profan'd,
See your most dreadful laws so loosely slighted,

---

71 easy: *trivial*   72 Lethe: *the river of oblivion*
73 use the person: *make use of my position as personal representative*
79 presented: *represented*   84 garland: *crown*
90 second body: *deputy*   92 propose: *imagine*

Behold yourself so by a son disdain'd;
And then imagine me taking your part, 96
And in your power soft silencing your son:
After this cold considerance, sentence me;
And, as you are a king, speak in your state
What I have done that misbecame my place, 100
My person, or my liege's sovereignty.
   Prince. You are right, justice; and you weigh this
     well;
Therefore still bear the balance and the sword:
And I do wish your honours may increase 104
Till you do live to see a son of mine
Offend you and obey you, as I did.
So shall I live to speak my father's words:
'Happy am I, that have a man so bold 108
That dares do justice on my proper son;
And not less happy, having such a son,
That would deliver up his greatness so
Into the hands of justice.' You did commit me: 112
For which, I do commit into your hand
The unstained sword that you have us'd to bear;
With this remembrance, that you use the same
With the like bold, just, and impartial spirit 116
As you have done 'gainst me. There is my hand:
You shall be as a father to my youth;
My voice shall sound as you do prompt mine ear,
And I will stoop and humble my intents 120
To your well-practis'd wise directions.
And, princes all, believe me, I beseech you;
My father is gone wild into his grave,
For in his tomb lie my affections; 124
And with his spirit sadly I survive,

98 considerance: *consideration*
103 balance and the sword: *emblems of Justice*
109 proper: *own*   115 remembrance: *admonition*
123, 124 *Cf. n.*   125 sadly: *soberly*

To mock the expectation of the world,
To frustrate prophecies, and to raze out
Rotten opinion, who hath writ me down   128
After my seeming. The tide of blood in me
Hath proudly flow'd in vanity till now:
Now doth it turn and ebb back to the sea,
Where it shall mingle with the state of floods 132
And flow henceforth in formal majesty.
Now call we our high court of parliament;
And let us choose such limbs of noble counsel,
That the great body of our state may go   136
In equal rank with the best govern'd nation;
That war or peace, or both at once, may be
As things acquainted and familiar to us;
In which you, father, shall have foremost hand. 140
Our coronation done, we will accite,
As I before remember'd, all our state:
And, God consigning to my good intents,
No prince nor peer shall have just cause to say, 144
God shorten Harry's happy life one day.   *Exeunt.*

Scene Three

[*The Garden of Justice Shallow's House in
Gloucestershire*]

*Enter Sir John, Shallow, Silence, Davy, Bardolph,
Page.*

   Shal. Nay, you shall see my orchard, where,
in an arbour, we will eat a last year's pippin of

129 After my seeming: *according to appearances*
132 state of floods: *majesty of the ocean*
137 In equal rank: *step by step*   141 accite: *summon*
142 remember'd: *mentioned*   143 consigning to: *confirming*

mine own graffing, with a dish of caraways, and
so forth; come, cousin Silence; and then to bed. 4

Fal. 'Fore God, you have here a goodly
dwelling, and a rich.

Shal. Barren, barren, barren; beggars all,
beggars all, Sir John: marry, good air. Spread, 8
Davy; spread: well said, Davy.

Fal. This Davy serves you for good uses; he
is your serving-man and your husband.

Shal. A good varlet, a good varlet, a very 12
good varlet, Sir John: by the mass, I have
drunk too much sack at supper: a good varlet.
Now sit down, now sit down. Come, cousin.

Sil. Ah, sirrah! quoth a', we shall   16

'Do nothing but eat, and make good cheer,
  And praise God for the merry year;
When flesh is cheap and females dear,
  And lusty lads roam here and there,   20
     So merrily.
And ever among so merrily.'

Fal. There's a merry heart! Good Master
Silence, I'll give you a health for that anon.   24

Shal. Give Master Bardolph some wine, Davy.

Davy. Sweet sir, sit; I'll be with you anon:
most sweet sir, sit. Master page, good master
page, sit. Proface! What you want in meat 28
we'll have in drink: but you must bear: the
heart's all.   [*Exit.*]

Shal. Be merry, Master Bardolph; and my
little soldier there, be merry.   32

3 graffing: *grafting*   caraways: *confection made with caraway seeds*
9 said: *done*   11 husband: *husbandman*
22 ever among: *all the while*
28 Proface: *may it do you good* (*Italian 'prò vi faccia'*)
30 heart: *intention*

Sil. 'Be merry, be merry, my wife has all;
  For women are shrews, both short and tall:
  'Tis merry in hall when beards wag all,
      And welcome merry Shrove-tide.   36
  Be merry, be merry.'

Fal. I did not think Master Silence had been
a man of this mettle.

Sil. Who, I?   I have been merry twice and 40
once ere now.

[*Enter Davy.*]

Davy. There's a dish of leather-coats for you.
        [*Setting them before Bardolph.*]

Shal. Davy!

Davy. Your worship! I'll be with you straight. 44
A cup of wine, sir?

Sil. 'A cup of wine that's brisk and fine
  And drink unto the leman mine;
      And a merry heart lives long-a.'   48

Fal. Well said, Master Silence.

Sil. And we shall be merry, now comes in the
sweet o' the night.

Fal. Health and long life to you, Master 52
Silence.

Sil. 'Fill the cup, and let it come;
  I'll pledge you a mile to the bottom.'

Shal. Honest Bardolph, welcome: if thou want- 56
est anything and wilt not call, beshrew thy heart.
[*To the Page.*] Welcome, my little tiny thief;
and welcome indeed too.   I'll drink to Master
Bardolph and to all the cavaleros about London. 60

36 Shrove-tide: *a time of special merriment at the close of the carnival*   42 leather-coats: *russet apples*
47 leman: *sweetheart*   60 cavaleros: *cavaliers*

Davy. I hope to see London once ere I die.

Bard. An I might see you there, Davy,—

Shal. By the mass, you'll crack a quart together: ha! will you not, Master Bardolph?   64

Bard. Yea, sir, in a pottle-pot.

Shal. By God's liggens, I thank thee. The
knave will stick by thee, I can assure thee that:
a' will not out; he is true bred.   68

Bard. And I'll stick by him, sir.

Shal. Why, there spoke a king. Lack nothing:
be merry.   [*One knocks at the door.*]
Look who's at door there. Ho! who knocks? 72
        [*Exit Davy.*]

Fal. [*To Silence, who drinks a bumper.*]
Why, now you have done me right.

Sil.   'Do me right,
            And dub me knight: 76
            Samingo.'

Is 't not so?

Fal. 'Tis so.

Sil. Is 't so? Why, then, say an old man can 80
do somewhat.

[Enter Davy.]

Davy. An 't please your worship, there's one
Pistol come from the court with news.

Fal. From the court! let him come in.   84

Enter Pistol.

How now, Pistol!

Pist. Sir John, God save you, sir!

66 liggens: *an original oath of Shallow's*
68 will not out: *will not fail (sporting term)*
74 done me right: *a common expression in drinking healths*
76 dub me knight; *cf. n.*
77 Samingo: *San Domingo, a common refrain in drinking songs*

Fal. What wind blew you hither, Pistol?

Pist. Not the ill wind which blows no man to good. 88

Sweet knight, thou art now one of the greatest men in this realm.

Sil. By 'r lady, I think a' be, but goodman Puff of Barson. 92

Pist. Puff!

Puff in thy teeth, most recreant coward base!

Sir John, I am thy Pistol and thy friend,

And helter-skelter have I rode to thee, 96

And tidings do I bring and lucky joys

And golden times and happy news of price.

Fal. I prithee now, deliver them like a man of this world.

Pist. A foutra for the world and worldlings base! 100

I speak of Africa and golden joys.

Fal. O base Assyrian knight, what is thy news?

Let King Cophetua know the truth thereof.

Sil. 'And Robin Hood, Scarlet, and John.' 104

Pist. Shall dunghill curs confront the Helicons?

And shall good news be baffled?

Then, Pistol, lay thy head in Furies' lap.

Shal. Honest gentleman, I know not your 108 breeding.

Pist. Why then, lament therefore.

Shal. Give me pardon, sir: if, sir, you come with news from the court, I take it there's but 112 two ways: either to utter them, or to conceal them. I am sir, under the king, in some authority.

91 but: *except* 92 Barson: *Barston in Warwickshire*
98 price: *value* 100 foutra: *exclamation of contempt*
103, 104 *These lines refer to popular ballads* 105 *Cf. n.*

Pist. Under which king, Bezonian? speak, or
die.   116
Shal. Under King Harry.
Pist.   Harry the Fourth? or Fifth?
Shal. Harry the Fourth.
Pist.   A foutra for thine office!
Sir John, thy tender lambkin now is king;
Harry the Fifth's the man. I speak the truth: 120
When Pistol lies, do this; and fig me, like
The bragging Spaniard.
   Fal. What! is the old king dead?
   Pist. As nail in door: the things I speak are
    just.   124
   Fal. Away, Bardolph! saddle my horse.
Master Robert Shallow, choose what office thou
wilt in the land, 'tis thine. Pistol, I will double
charge thee with dignities.   128
   Bard. O joyful day!
I would not take a knighthood for my fortune.
   Pist. What! I do bring good news.
   Fal. Carry Master Silence to bed. Master 132
Shallow, my Lord Shallow, be what thou wilt, I
am Fortune's steward. Get on thy boots: we'll
ride all night. O sweet Pistol! Away, Bardolph!
[*Exit Bardolph.*] Come, Pistol, utter more to 136
me; and withal devise something to do thyself
good. Boot, boot, Master Shallow: I know the
young king is sick for me. Let us take any
man's horses; the laws of England are at my 140
commandment. Blessed are they which have
been my friends, and woe to my lord chief
justice!

115 Bezonian: *base beggar*
121 fig: *to thrust the thumb between two closed fingers, or into the
    mouth, a vulgar insult, imported from Spain*
124 just: *correct*

Pist. Let vultures vile seize on his lungs also! 144
'Where is the life that late I led?' say they:
Why, here it is: welcome these pleasant days!
Exeunt.

Scene Four

[*London. A Street*]

Enter Hostess Quickly, Doll Tearsheet, and Beadles.

Host. No, thou arrant knave: I would to God
that I might die that I might have thee hanged;
thou hast drawn my shoulder out of joint.

First Bead. The   constables   have   delivered 4
her over to me, and she shall have whipping-
cheer enough, I warrant her: there hath been a
man or two lately killed about her.

Dol. Nut-hook, nut-hook, you lie. Come on; 8
I'll tell thee what, thou damned tripe-visaged
rascal, an the child I now go with do miscarry,
thou wert better thou hadst struck thy mother,
thou paper-faced villain.   12

Host. O the Lord! that Sir John were come;
he would make this a bloody day to somebody.
But I pray God the fruit of her womb miscarry!

First Bead. If it do, you shall have a dozen 16
of cushions again; you have but eleven now.
Come, I charge you both go with me; for the man
is dead that you and Pistol beat amongst you.

Dol. I'll tell you what, you thin man in a 20
censer, I will have you as soundly swinged for

145 *Quotation from another ballad*
8 nut-hook: *slang for beadle; cf. catchpole*
20, 21 in a censer: *i.e., a figure embossed on a censer*
21 swinged: *whipped*

this, you blue-bottle rogue! you filthy famished
correctioner! if you be not swinged, I'll forswear half-kirtles.   24

First Bead. Come, come, you she knight-errant,
come.

Host. O God, that right should thus overcome
might! Well, of sufferance comes ease.

Dol. Come, you rogue, come: bring me to 28
a justice.

Host. Ay; come, you starved blood-hound.

Dol. Goodman death! goodman bones!

Host. Thou atomy, thou!   32

Dol. Come, you thin thing; come, you rascal!

First Bead. Very well.   *Exeunt.*

Scene Five

[*A public Place near Westminster Abbey*]

    Enter two Grooms, strewers of rushes.

First Groom. More rushes, more rushes.

Sec. Groom. The trumpets have sounded
twice.

First Groom. 'Twill be two o'clock ere they 4
come from the coronation. Dispatch, dispatch.
                         Exeunt Grooms.

*Trumpets sound, and the King and his train pass
    over the stage. After them, enter Falstaff,
    Shallow, Pistol, Bardolph, and the Boy.*

Fal. Stand here by me, Master Robert Shallow; I will make the king do you grace. I will

22 blue-bottle: *the reference is to the beadle's blue livery*
24 half-kirtles: *waists or skirts*   27 of sufferance: *out of suffering*
32 atomy: *Dame Quickly's confusion of 'atom' with 'anatomy' =
skeleton*

leer upon him, as a' comes by; and do but mark 8
the countenance that he will give me.

Pist. God bless thy lungs, good knight.

Fal. Come here, Pistol; stand behind me.
O! if I had had time to have made new liveries, 12
I would have bestowed the thousand pound I
borrowed of you. But 'tis no matter; this poor
show doth better: this doth infer the zeal I had
to see him.   16

Shal. It doth so.

Fal. It shows my earnestness of affection.

Shal. It doth so.

Fal. My devotion.   20

Shal. It doth, it doth, it doth.

Fal. As it were, to ride day and night; and
not to deliberate, not to remember, not to have
patience to shift me.   24

Shal. It is best, certain.

Fal. But to stand stained with travel, and
sweating with desire to see him; thinking of
nothing else; putting all affairs else in oblivion, 28
as if there were nothing else to be done but to
see him.

Pist. 'Tis *semper idem,* for *absque hoc nihil est:*
'Tis all in every part.   32

Shal. 'Tis so, indeed.

Pist. My knight, I will inflame thy noble liver,
And make thee rage.
Thy Doll, and Helen of thy noble thoughts,   36
Is in base durance and contagious prison;
Hal'd thither
By most mechanical and dirty hand:

31, 32 *Cf. n.*   39 mechanical: *common, vulgar*

Rouse up revenge from ebon den with fell Alecto's
    snake,   40
For Doll is in: Pistol speaks nought but truth.
    Fal. I will deliver her.
             [Shouts within and trumpets sound.]
  Pist. There roar'd the sea, and trumpet-clangour
    sounds.

*The trumpets sound.   Enter King Henry the Fifth,
    Brothers, Lord Chief Justice.*

    Fal. God save thy grace, King Hal! my royal 44
Hal!
    Pist. The heavens thee guard and keep, most
royal imp of fame!
    Fal. God save thee, my sweet boy!   48
    K. Hen. V. My lord chief justice, speak to that
vain man.
    Ch. Just. Have you your wits? know you what 'tis
you speak?
    Fal. My king! my Jove! I speak to thee, my
heart!
    K. Hen. V. I know thee not, old man: fall to thy
    prayers;   52
How ill white hairs become a fool and jester!
I have long dream'd of such a kind of man,
So surfeit-swell'd, so old, and so profane;
But, being awak'd, I do despise my dream.   56
Make less thy body hence, and more thy grace;
Leave gormandising; know the grave doth gape
For thee thrice wider than for other men.
Reply not to me with a fool-born jest: 60
Presume not that I am the thing I was;
For God doth know, so shall the world perceive,

40 ebon: *black*   Alecto: *one of the Furies*
47 imp: *child*   49 vain: *foolish*

That I have turn'd away my former self;
So will I those that kept me company.   64
When thou dost hear I am as I have been,
Approach me, and thou shalt be as thou wast,
The tutor and the feeder of my riots:
Till then, I banish thee, on pain of death,   68
As I have done the rest of my misleaders,
Not to come near our person by ten mile.
For competence of life I will allow you,
That lack of means enforce you not to evil: 72
And, as we hear you do reform yourselves,
We will, according to your strength and qualities,
Give you advancement. Be it your charge, my lord,
To see perform'd the tenour of our word.   76
Set on.   *Exit the King [with his Train].*

Fal. Master Shallow, I owe you a thousand pound.

Shal. Yea, marry, Sir John; which I beseech
you to let me have home with me.   80

Fal. That can hardly be, Master Shallow. Do
not you grieve at this: I shall be sent for in
private to him. Look you, he must seem thus
to the world. Fear not your advancements; I 84
will be the man yet that shall make you great.

Shal. I cannot perceive how, unless you give
me your doublet and stuff me out with straw.
I beseech you, good Sir John, let me have five 88
hundred of my thousand.

Fal. Sir, I will be as good as my word: this
that you heard was but a colour.

Shal. A colour that I fear you will die in, Sir 92
John.

Fal. Fear no colours: go with me to dinner.

92 colour: *pun on collar, halter*
94 Fear no colours: *have no fear; originally, fear no enemy*

Come, Lieutenant Pistol; come, Bardolph: I
shall be sent for soon at night.   96

Enter Justice and Prince John.

Ch. Just. Go, carry Sir John Falstaff to the Fleet;
Take all his company along with him.
   Fal. My lord, my lord!
   Ch. Just. I cannot now speak: I will hear you
   soon.   100
Take them away.
   Pist. Si fortuna me tormenta, spero contenta.
         Exeunt. Mane[n]t [Prince John of] Lancaster
                              and Chief Justice.
   Lanc. I like this fair proceeding of the king's.
He hath intent his wonted followers   104
Shall all be very well provided for;
But all are banish'd till their conversations
Appear more wise and modest to the world.
   Ch. Just. And so they are.   108
   Lanc. The king hath call'd his parliament, my
   lord.
   Ch. Just. He hath.
   Lanc. I will lay odds, that, ere this year expire,
We bear our civil swords and native fire   112
As far as France. I heard a bird so sing,
Whose music, to my thinking, pleas'd the king.
Come, will you hence?   *Exeunt.*

97 the Fleet: *a London prison*   106 conversations: *habits*

EPILOGUE

[Spoken by a Dancer.]

First, my fear; then, my curtsy; last my
speech. My fear is, your displeasure, my
curtsy, my duty, and my speech, to beg your
pardon. If you look for a good speech now, you   4
undo me; for what I have to say is of mine
own making; and what indeed I should say
will, I doubt, prove mine own marring. But to
the purpose, and so to the venture. Be it known   8
to you,—as it is very well,—I was lately here in
the end of a displeasing play, to pray your
patience for it and to promise you a better. I
did mean indeed to pay you with this; which, 12
if like an ill venture it come unluckily home, I
break, and you, my gentle creditors, lose. Here,
I promised you I would be, and here I commit
my body to your mercies: bate me some and I 16
will pay you some; and, as most debtors do,
promise you infinitely.

If my tongue cannot entreat you to acquit me,
will you command me to use my legs? and yet 20
that were but light payment, to dance out of your
debt. But a good conscience will make any
possible satisfaction, and so will I. All the
gentlewomen here have forgiven me: if the 24
gentlemen will not, then the gentlemen do not
agree with the gentlewomen, which was never
seen before in such an assembly.

One word more, I beseech you. If you be not 28
too much cloyed with fat meat, our humble

author will continue the story, with Sir John in
it, and make you merry with fair Katharine of
France: where, for anything I know, Falstaff 32
shall die of a sweat, unless already a' be killed
with your hard opinions; for Oldcastle died a
martyr, and this is not the man. My tongue is
weary; when my legs are too, I will bid you 36
good night: and so kneel down before you; but,
indeed, to pray for the queen.

38 to pray for the queen; *cf. n.*

NOTES.

Ind. S. d. *Rumour, painted full of tongues.* Vergil (*Æneid* iv. 174) describes Fame, or Rumour, as covered with ears, eyes, and tongues. Cf. also Chaucer, *Hous of Fame,* 1389-90.

Ind. 24. *Shrewsbury.* The last act of Shakespeare's *Henry IV, Part I,* is devoted to the battle of Shrewsbury, in which the King and his armies overcome the rebel forces under young Harry Percy (Hotspur); his uncle, the Earl of Worcester; and the Scottish Earl of Douglas.

Ind. 29. *Harry Monmouth.* Henry, Prince of Wales, who, according to Shakespeare, killed Hotspur in single combat at the battle of Shrewsbury. Monmouth was the place of his birth.

Ind. 35. *hole.* Shakespeare is obviously playing on the words *hole* and *hold.* Most modern editors have spoiled the rather poor pun by substituting the word *hold* for *hole.*

I. i. 116-118. 'By his spirit was his party inspired, i.e., made keen and sharp as steel; but, when once his spirit was brought down (technically, reduced to a lower temper) all his followers became dull and heavy as lead.'

I. i. 128. In *1 Henry IV,* V. iii., Douglas kills Sir Walter Blunt, who was dressed to resemble the King, and tells us that he has already killed the Lord of Stafford in the king's 'likeness.' When, later, Prince Hal challenges Douglas to single combat, he says:

'the spirits
Of valiant Shirley, Stafford, Blunt, are in my arms.'

I. i. 166-179. These lines are the first of a series of passages omitted in the Quarto texts of the play

and added by the Folio. The other important Folio
additions are the following: I. i. 189-209; I. iii. 21-
24; I. iii. 36-55; I. iii. 85-108; II. iii. 23-45; IV. i.
55-79; Epilogue 37, 38 (and so kneel . . . queen).
Furthermore, the whole of III. i., containing the
King's famous soliloquy on sleep, is omitted in certain Quarto copies, though added in others. On the
other hand, certain passages, usually shorter and
belonging to the prose scenes, are omitted in the
Folio version; viz., I. ii. 244-251 (But it was . . .
motion); II. ii. 26-31 (and God . . . strengthened);
II. iv. 14, 15 (Dispatch . . . straight); II. iv. 144-
146; II. iv. 428 f. (Come! . . . come, Doll?); III.
i. 53-56 (O! . . . die); III. ii. 340, 341 (yet lecherous . . . mandrake); III. ii. 342-345 (and sung
. . . good-nights); IV. i. 93; IV. i. 95.

I. i. 204, 205. According to Shakespeare, King
Richard II, predecessor and cousin of Henry IV,
was murdered in Pomfret castle at Henry's hint,
after the latter had forced Richard's abdication. Cf.
Shakespeare's *Richard II*. Richard Scroop, Archbishop of York, belonged to a family which was
firmly attached to the cause of Richard.

I. i. 208. *Bolingbroke*. King Henry, born in
Bolingbroke castle, Lincolnshire.

I. ii. 18. *manned with an agate*. Attended by a
servant as small as a figure cut in an agate.

I. ii. 25. *face-royal*. A royal was a gold coin
worth ten shillings. Falstaff is here playing on the
double sense of a 'royal face' and the face stamped
on the coin.

I. ii. 38. *glutton*. The parable of Dives and
Lazarus (St. Luke 16, 19-31) is frequently referred
to by Falstaff, possibly because Dives, 'the glutton,'
who 'fared sumptuously every day,' but who went to
hell and called out for the poor man Lazarus to 'dip
the tip of his finger in water and cool my tongue,'

reminds Falstaff of his own manner of life and probable fate.

I. ii. 39. *Achitophel.* The counsellor of Absalom (II Samuel 15-17) who was cursed by David, and who 'gat him home to his house and hanged himself' after Absalom rejected his counsel.

I. ii. 40. *yea-forsooth knave.* The reference is to the mild oaths employed by the Puritanical middle-class tradespeople of Shakespeare's own day. Cf. Hotspur's ridicule of this same trait in *1 Henry IV*, III. i. 251 ff.

I. ii. 51-54. Falstaff is here playing with the ancient jest that deceived husbands wear invisible horns. Lightness is obviously used in a double sense, and the old spelling of lanthorn, which emphasizes the horn sides of an Elizabethan lantern, carries out the jest.

I. ii. 57. *Paul's.* The nave of St. Paul's Cathedral was in Shakespeare's day the business center of London. From eleven to twelve, and three to six, daily, men of all professions and trades congregated there. Men out of work, and masters looking for servants, posted their advertisements on the pillars of the nave. Falstaff is probably referring here to a popular saying, quoted in *The Choice of Change,* 1598: 'A man must not make choice of three things in three places: of a wife in Westminster, of a servant in Paul's, of a horse in Smithfield; lest he choose a quean, a knave, or a jade.' Smithfield is the great cattle market of London.

I. ii. 61, 62. This episode from *The Famous Victories of Henry V* is reprinted in Appendix A, see pp. 142, 143.

I. ii. 102. *hunt counter.* A hunting term meaning to follow the trail in a direction opposite to that which the game has taken. There is also perhaps here a pun on the two Compters, or debtors', prisons in London.

I. ii. 166-168. Blind beggars often had dogs to lead them through the streets.

I. ii. 182. *wax.* 'A poor quibble on the word wax, which signifies increase as well as the matter of the honey-comb.' Johnson.

I. ii. 189-192. An angel was a gold coin, worth upwards of six shillings, which took its name from its device, the archangel Michael. Falstaff is here punning on the word, and in the phrases *cannot go* and *cannot tell,* he is perhaps using terms which refer to the circulation of money, meaning 'I cannot pass current. I cannot count as good coin.'

I. ii. 241. *spit white.* Furnivall quotes *Batman uppon Bartholome* (1582): 'If the spettle be white viscus, the sicknesse cometh of fleame; if black, of melancholy;—the white spettle not knottie, signifieth health.'

I. ii. 257. *bear crosses.* Another quibble on coins, many of which were marked with crosses.

I. ii. 259. A three-man beetle is a mallet so heavy that it requires three men to swing it. *Filliping the toad,* according to Steevens, is a Warwickshire game, in which a toad is placed on the end of a short board placed across a log; the other end of the board is then struck with a mallet, and the toad thrown into the air. If Falstaff took the part of the toad in this game, it would, he implies, require a three-man beetle to fillip one of his size.

I. iii. 36-41. Many emendations have been suggested for this apparently corrupt passage. It is probable that a line has been lost here, but it is possible to understand Lord Bardolph's speech without changing the text. Lord Hastings has just been remonstrating with Lord Bardolph for his pessimism, saying that hope never injured any cause. Lord

Bardolph replies: 'Yes, it does,—if, for example, this present business of war (indeed this very action now contemplated, this cause that is now on foot), lives merely on such desperate hopes as buds which appear too early in the spring; for hope gives less warrant that these buds will become fruit than despair gives that the frosts will destroy them.'

I. iii. 53-55. 'Know how well able our estate is to undergo such a work, and how well able it is to balance the power of our opponent.'

II. i. 36, 37.   When Dame Quickly says, 'A hundred mark is a long one,' i.e., a long mark, score, or reckoning, she puns on a hundred marks as a debt and a hundred yard mark at archery.

II. i. 67, 68.   *rampallian.* Elizabethan slang, rascal, rapscallion; used also by Beaumont and Fletcher. *Fustilarian,* a word coined by Falstaff, suggested by the word *fustilugs,* a fat, frowsy woman. *Catastrophe,* in the sense of conclusion, end; used jocularly here for the posteriors.

II. i. 145.   Falstaff has the legal right to demand protection against the just claims of Mistress Quickly, as he is about to set forth for the north on the King's business. The Chief Justice admits his 'power to do wrong' in this matter, but urges him to answer the poor woman's suit in a manner suitable to his reputation as a gentleman and soldier.

II. i. 159.   Falstaff tries to comfort Mistress Quickly for the loss of her plate by assuring her that glasses are much more fashionable and pleasanter to drink from than silver goblets.

II. i. 210.   'This is the proper behaviour in fencing.' Falstaff refers to his inattention to the Justice's remarks as a retaliation for the Justice's inattention to his questions in ll. 184 ff.

II. ii. 25-31.   Shirts were made of holland linen

(worth 'eight shillings an ell,' cf. *1 Henry IV*, III. iii. 83). The play on the words holland and low-countries is apparent. The Prince proceeds to assume that Poins's shortage in shirts is due to the fact that his old shirts are serving as garments for his illegitimate children, who 'bawl out' from 'the ruins of his linen.'

II. ii. 95-100. Either Shakespeare or the Page confuses the dream of Hecuba with that of Althea. Althea dreamed that the Fates told her that her new-born son would live only so long as a burning brand on the hearth remained unconsumed. Althea snatched the brand from the hearth, extinguished the fire, and prolonged her son's life.

II. ii. 112. *martlemas.* Corrupted form of Martinmas, or the Feast of St. Martin, November 11. This day was considered the last day of autumn, and was also the day for salting and hanging the winter's supply of beef. The reference is obviously to Falstaff's hearty old age (cf. *All-hallown summer, 1 Henry IV*, I. ii. 177, note), or to Falstaff as a 'martlemas beef.'

II. ii. 127, 128. *borrower's cap.* A man asking for a loan is always very ready to take off his cap.

II. ii. 130 ff. Most modern editors have rearranged the following speeches, giving to Poins the reading of Falstaff's letter to Hal. The Quarto and Folio arrangement, followed with one exception (cf. Appendix C) in this text, seems more natural. In lines 109, 110 Bardolph evidently gives the letter to the Prince, not to Poins. In line 119 the Prince shows the letter to Poins, but does not necessarily give it to him.

II. ii. 192, 193. The parallel is not striking. Jove took the form of a bull to woo Europa. Hal disguises himself as a waiter to spy upon Falstaff. The leather jerkins are the only connecting link.

II. iv. 36.   The ballad sung by Falstaff has been preserved in Percy's *Reliques*.

II. iv. 52.   Another scrap of an old ballad.

II. iv. 91.   *debuty.*   Mistress Quickly's pronunciation of deputy, and of Wednesday in line 93, both of which are corrected in the Folio text, indicates that she has a cold in her head.

II. iv. 104, 105.   *tame cheater.*   A cant term for a low gamester, especially for a gamester's decoy. Mistress Quickly understands the word in the sense of escheator, or officer of the exchequer.   The Cambridge editors suggest the emendation *chetah,* the hunting leopard, known in Europe as early as the fifteenth century.   The sentence, *you may stroke him as gently as a puppy greyhound,* would indicate at least that Falstaff is playing on the two words *cheater* and *chetah.*   One would hardly speak of stroking a gamester's decoy.

II. iv. 159.   *occupy.*   This word was used only in an obscene sense in Shakespeare's day.   From the sixteenth to the nineteenth century it seldom appears in literature.

II. iv. 172.   *Have we not Hiren here?*   This phrase, which became proverbial in Elizabethan drama, probably originated in a lost play by George Peele, entitled, *The Turkish Mahomet and Hyren* (Irene) *the Fair Greek.*   Pistol applies the name to his sword.   Mistress Quickly (ll. 189, 190) thinks he is inquiring for some woman.

II. iv. 177, 178.   Pistol misquotes from Marlowe's *Tamburlaine the Great, Pt. II,* IV, iv:

> 'Holla, ye pamper'd jades of Asia!
> What! can ye draw but twenty miles a day?'

II. iv. 192.   Another burlesque of contemporary drama.   This time Shakespeare puts into Pistol's mouth a reference to Peele's *Battle of Alcazar,* printed in 1594, in which Muley Mahomet enters with lion's flesh on his sword, which he offers to his wife with the words,

'Feed then and faint not, my fair Calypolis.'

II. iv. 194.   Most editors assume that Pistol is speaking bad Italian.   The Cambridge editors suggest that it is perhaps bad Spanish, and that he is reading the motto on his Toledo blade.   Douce gives an illustration of a sword with a French version of this motto inscribed upon it.   Farmer says: 'Pistol is only a copy of Hannibal Gonsaga who vaunted on yielding himself a prisoner, as you may read in an old collection of tales called *Wits, Fits, Fancies:*

Si Fortuna me tormenta
Il speranza me contenta.'

Whatever the language, the meaning of Pistol's motto is, If Fortune torments me, Hope contents me.

II. iv. 205.   *shove-groat shilling.*   Shove-groat was a game which was a cross between shuffle-board and 'pitching pennies.'   It was played on a board three feet long and a foot wide, and the object of the players was to shove coins into numbered spaces at the far end of the board.

II. iv. 267.   *drinks . . . flapdragons.*   Flapdragon or snapdragon is a sport which consists in snapping raisins or grapes from burning brandy and eating them.

II. iv. 286.   An impossible conjunction of planets.

II. iv. 288.   *fiery Trigon.*   Poins continues the astrological figure by referring to the red-nosed Bardolph as the fiery Trigon.   When the three superior planets were in that division of the zodiac which consisted of the three so-called fiery signs, Aries, Leo, and Sagittarius, they were said to be in the fiery Trigon, or triangle; when they were in Cancer,

Scorpio, and Pisces, they were in the watery Trigon, etc.

II. iv. 363. *dead elm.* Shakespeare mentions elms three times,—here and in *The Comedy of Errors,* II. ii. 176, and in *A Midsummer Night's Dream,* IV. i. 49. In both *C. of E.* and *M. N. D.* the reference is to the practice of training ivy on elm trees, illustrating the relation of woman to man. Poins is therefore probably referring to the posture of Falstaff and Doll.

III. ii. 28, 29. Sir John Oldcastle and Sir John Fastolfe, with both of whom Falstaff has been identified (cf. *1 Henry IV,* this edition, Appendix C 3), were both pages to the Duke of Norfolk in their youth.

III. ii. 33. *Skogan.* Shakespeare probably took the name from a jest book published in 1565, called *Scogin's Jests.* This Scogin was the court fool of King Edward IV. It is possible, however, that the reference is to Chaucer's friend, Henry Scogan, described by Ben Jonson in *The Fortunate Isles* as 'a fine gentieman, and master of arts, of Henry the Fourth's time.'

III. ii. 73. *accommodated.* This is one of the words which Ben Jonson (*Discoveries*) refers to as one of 'the perfumed terms of the time.' Bardolph is giving himself airs and imitating the affectations of fashionable gallants.

III. ii. 239. Bullcalf means to say: 'Here, in French crowns, is the equivalent of four English ten-shilling pieces, or ten-shilling pieces with King Henry's head on them.' As a matter of fact Henry VII was the first English king whose head appeared on ten shilling pieces.

III. ii. 264. *three pound.* Falstaff's followers adopt his own methods. Bardolph has collected four pounds, forty shillings from each of the two men, but decides to keep a commission of twenty-five per cent.

III. ii. 285. *gibbets*. A brewer's gibbet was the yoke worn across the shoulders for carrying buckets of beer from the vat to the barrels. Falstaff refers to the dexterity with which brewers' men swing the buckets on to the gibbet.

III. ii. 301-303. Sir Dagonet was King Arthur's fool. Arthur's show was an exhibition of archery held annually at Mile-end Green by a society called The Auncient Order, Societie, and Unitie laudable of Prince Arthur and his Knightly Armoury of the Round Table. There were fifty-eight members and each took the name of one of the knights in the old romances.

III. ii. 346. *Vice's dagger*. The Vice, a character in the old Morality plays, carried a thin wooden dagger.

III. ii. 357. *philosopher's two stones*. The philosophers' stone is the reputed stone of the alchemists which transmutes base metals into gold. Falstaff decides that Justice Shallow will be as valuable to him as two philosophers' stones!

IV. i. 94-96. This passage is obviously corrupt. The archbishop means in general: 'I make this my quarrel on both public and private grounds, that is, because of the sufferings of the commonwealth and of my own family at the hands of King Henry.' The Archbishop's brother, an adherent of King Richard, had been executed by King Henry's order; cf. *1 Henry IV*, I. iii. 270.

IV. i. 117 ff. This contest is described in the first act of Shakespeare's *Richard II*.

IV. i. 175. *consign'd*. The Quarto and Folio read confin'd; consign'd is Johnson's emendation. The meaning seems to be that the terms of surrender in-

clude the stipulation that the execution of the wishes
of the rebels shall be consigned to their own hands.

IV. ii. Shakespeare evidently had no thought of
a change of scene, or of pause in action, here. Even
the first Folio has no stage direction of exeunt at
the end of Scene i., and no indication of scene division. I have kept the conventional modern arrangement for convenience of reference; but the reader
should remember that the Archbishop and his party
do not leave the stage,—they merely step forward
to greet Prince John as he enters.

IV. iii. 125. *a mere hoard of gold kept by a devil.*
Falstaff refers to the old superstition that gold mines
were guarded by devils.

IV. iv. S. d. *The Jerusalem Chamber.* An apart-
ment adjoining the southwest tower of Westminster
Abbey, built in the fourteenth century as a guest-
chamber, and deriving its name from the tapestries
depicting the history of Jerusalem with which it was
hung. Since the seventeenth century it has been
used as a council chamber.

IV. iv. 33-35. 'Nevertheless when he is incensed
he breaks out in fiery fashion like flint; he abounds
in caprices as winter abounds in moisture; and he
changes his moods as suddenly as water freezes and
melts at the edge of a pond at daybreak.' *Flaws*
are the blades of ice seen on the edges of water on
winter mornings.

IV. iv. 44-48. 'That the vessel of their united
blood may never leak, even though that blood should
be mingled with the venom caused by hints and sug-
gestions tending toward discord, which in this age
will be sure to be poured in; and even though this
venom should work with the strength of aconite or
gunpowder.'

IV. iv. 79, 80. 'It seldom happens that the bee,
having deposited her comb in dead carrion, leaves the

comb and the carrion.' The application is to the
Prince and his low company.

IV. v. 161. *medicine potable.* 'There has long
prevailed an opinion that a solution of gold has
great medicinal virtues, and that the incorruptibility
of gold might be communicated to the body impreg-
nated with it.' Johnson.

IV. v. 198. *mode.* The key in which music is
written, used figuratively and associated with 'mood'
in the sense of state of mind.

V. i. 1. *cock and pie.* The origin of this common
Elizabethan oath is obscure. Cock is probably a
corruption of God, as in the oath Cock's wounds;
and pie is perhaps the Roman service book which
was sometimes so called, though the word pie applies
more properly to the index of the service book. By
Shakespeare's time the meaning of the oath was forgotten, and Justice Shallow doubtless thinks he is
swearing by a cock and a magpie.

V. ii. 34. 'Which goes against the grain with one
in your position.'

V. ii. 48. This allusion helps to fix the date of the
play. Amurath the Fourth succeeded his father on
the Turkish throne in 1596. Upon his accession he
invited his brothers to dinner and had them all
strangled.

V. ii. 123, 124. This strange remark of the Prince
seems to mean that inasmuch as his own wild affections and desires died at the moment of his father's
death, they are now, as it were, buried with his
father. Hence his father may be said to be buried
with wild affections, or to have 'gone wild into his
grave.'

V. iii. 76. *dub me knight.* The reference is to the
Elizabethan custom of giving the title of knight for
the evening to a man who, kneeling to his mistress,
drained a mighty bumper to her health.

V. iii. 105. Helicon was the abode of the Muses. Pistol resents having such low fellows as Robin Hood and his men brought into this very grandiloquent literary conversation.

V. v. 31, 32. Pistol quotes two Latin phrases which have no significance here, and then proceeds to mistranslate them. The Latin means literally: it is always the same, for without this there is nothing.

Epil. Shakespeare's authorship of this epilogue has been questioned. The dancer says it is of his own making, but he speaks for the author in promising a continuation of the play and in assuring the audience that Falstaff is not Sir John Oldcastle (cf. note on III. ii. 28, 29, and Appendix C 3 to *1 Henry IV,* in the present edition). It is interesting to note that Shakespeare's original intention was to continue the Falstaff plot through the play of *Henry V;* but, as Coleridge remarks, 'Agincourt is not the place for the splendid mendacity of Falstaff. With the coronation of Henry V opens a new period of glorious enthusiasm and patriotic fervor. There is no longer any place for Falstaff on earth; he must find refuge in "Arthur's bosom."'

Epil. 38. *pray for the queen.* It was the custom to end plays with a prayer for the sovereign. This custom originated in the interludes.

APPENDIX A

SOURCES OF THE PLAY

The principal source of the main plot of this play is the 1587 edition of *The Chronicles of England, Scotland, and Ireland,* by Raphael Holinshed. Samuel Daniel's poem, *The Civill Wars of England* (1595), or its source, may well have had some influence. Several incidents in the comic plot are taken, apparently, from the play *The Famous Victories of Henry V,* first acted in 1588, licensed in 1594, and published in 1598.

Holinshed's Chronicle

According to Holinshed, the Earl of Northumberland was pardoned by the king after the battle of Shrewsbury in 1403. But in 1405 when 'the king was minded to haue gone into Wales against the rebels that vnder their cheeftane Owen Glendower ceassed not to doo much mischeef against the English subiects,' he was 'further disquieted' by a 'conspiracie put in practise against him at home by the Earle of Northumberland who had conspired with Richard Scroope, Archbishop of Yorke, Thomas Mowbraie earle marshall,' and others. 'The King aduertised of these matters left his iournie into Wales and marched with all speed toward the north parts. Also Rafe Neuill earl of Westmerland, that was not farre off, together with the lord Iohn of Lancaster, the king's sonne, being informed of this rebellious attempt, assembled togither such power as they might make . . . made forward against the rebels, and coming into a plaine within the forrest of Galtree caused their standards to be pitched downe in the like sort as the Archbishop had pitched his ouer against them, being farre stronger in number of people than the other, for as some write there were of the rebels at least twentie thousand men.'

Shakespeare follows Holinshed closely in describing the 'subtill policie' whereby the rebels are disposed of; but he transfers the odium attaching to this action from the earl of Westmoreland to Lord John of Lancaster.

The events of the next eight years, as related by Holinshed, are unnoticed in the play. Shakespeare proceeds immediately to the death of the king, and again follows the Chronicle closely. '1413. The morrow after Candlemas daie began a parlement which the king had called at London, but he departed this life before the same parlement was ended; for now that his prouisions were readie and that he was furnished with sufficient treasure, soldiers, capteins, vittels, munitions, tall ships, strong gallies, and all things necessarie for such a roiall iournie as he pretended to take into the holie land, he was eftsoones taken with a sore sicknesse, which was not a leprosie striken by the hand of God, as foolish friars imagined, but a verie apoplexie. . . . During this sicknesse he caused his crowne to be set on a pillow at his bed's head, and suddenlie his pangs so sore troubled him that he laie as though all his vitall spirits had beene from him departed. Such as were about him couered his face with a linen cloth. The prince, his sonne, being hereof aduertised, entered into the chamber, tooke awaie the crowne, and departed. The father being suddenlie reuiued out of that trance quicklie perceiued the lacke of his crowne; and hauing knowledge that the prince his sonne had taken it awaie caused him to come before his presence requiring of him what he meant so to misuse himself. The prince with a good audacitie answered, Sir, to mine and all mens iudgements you seemed dead in this world, wherefore I as youre next heire apparent tooke that as mine owne, and not as yours. Well, faire sonne, said the king with a great sigh, what right I had to it God knoweth. Well, said the prince, if you die king, I will haue the garland and trust to keepe it with the sword against all mine enemies as you haue done. Then said the king, I commit all to God, and remember you to doo well. With that he turned himself in his bed and shortlie after departed to God in a chamber of the abbats of Westminster called Ierusalem, . . . when he had reigned thirteene yeares in great perplexitie and little pleasure.'

Holinshed then tells us that 'king Henrie the fift was crowned the ninth of Aprill, being Passion Sundaie, which was a sore, ruggie, and tempestuous daie, with wind, snow, and sleet, that men greatlie maruelled thereat, making diuerse interpretations what that might signifie. But this king, to show that in his person princelie honors should change publike manners, he determined to put on him the shape of a new man. For whereas aforetime he had made himself a companion vnto misrulie mates of dissolute order and life, he now banished them all from his presence, but not vnrewarded or else vnpreferred, inhibiting them vpon a great paine not once to approach, lodge, or soiourne within ten miles of his court or presence: and in their places he chose men of grauitie, wit, and high policie, by whose wise councel he might at all times rule to his honor and dignity; calling to mind how once to hie offence of the king his father he had with his fist striken the cheefe iustice for sending one of his minions, vpon desert, to prison, when the iustice stoutlie commanded himself also streict to ward, and the prince obeied.'

Daniel's Civill Wars

In the fourth book of his *Civill Wars,* Daniel condenses history even more radically than Shakespeare.

The king falls sick immediately after his victory at
Shrewsbury, and is afflicted by spectres of Conscience
and Death. He commands

> 'some that attending were
> To fetch the crowne and set it in his sight;
> On which with fixed eye and heauie cheere
> Casting a looke, O God, sayeth he, what right
> I had to thee my soule doth now conceiue,—
> Thee which with blood I got, with horror leave.'

Horror so overwhelms the king that he swoons—

> 'When loe his Sonne comes in and takes away
> The fatall crowne from thence and out he goes
> As if unwilling longer time to lose.'

The king revives, summons the prince, and says:

> 'O sonne, what needes thee make such speed
> Vnto that care where feare exceedes thy right,
> And when his sinne whom thou shalt now succeed
> Shall still upbraide thy inheritance of might?
> And if thou canst liue, and liue great, from woe,
> Without this carefull trauaille, let it goe.'

The prince replies:

> 'What wrong hath not continuance quite outworne?
> Yeeres make that right which neuer was so borne.'

The king dies praying that virtuous deeds and the
holy wars of his son may atone for his own sins.

The Famous Victories of Henry V

In this crude play Prince Hal is twice committed
to prison, once by the Lord Mayor for rioting in
the streets after a merry evening at the tavern in
Eastcheap, and once by the Lord Chief Justice for
giving him 'a box on the ear' upon his refusal to
pardon one of the prince's companions who has been
convicted of highway robbery.

The following are characteristic selections:

Enter Henry the fourth, with the earle of Exeter and the earle of Oxford.

Oxf. Please your maiestie, heere is my Lord maior and the sheriffe of London.

King Hen. 4. Admit them to our presence.

Enter the Maior and the Sheriffe.

   Now, my good Lord Maior of London, the cause of my sending to you at this time is to tel you of a matter which I have learned of my councell: Herein I understand that you haue committed my sonne to prison without our leaue and license. What although he be a rude youth and likely to give occasion, yet you might haue considered that he is a Prince and my sonne, and not to be halled to prison by euery subiect.

Maior. May it please your maiestie to give us leaue to tell our tale.

King Hen. 4. Or else God forbid, otherwise you might think me an vnequall Iudge, hauing more affection to my sonne then to any rightfull iudgement.

Maior. Then if it please your Maiestie, this night betwixt two and three of the clocke of the morning, my Lord the young Prince with a very disordered companie, came to the olde Tauerne in Eastcheape, and whether it was that their Musicke liked them not, or whether they were ouercome with wine, I know not, but they drew their swords and into the street they went, and some toke my Lord the yong Princes part, and some tooke the other, but betwixt them there was such a bloodie fray for the space of half an houre, that neither watchmen nor any other could stay them, till my brother the Sheriffe of London and I were sent for, and at the laste with much adoo we staied them, but it was long first, which was a great disquieting to all your louing subiects there-

abouts: and then my good Lord, we knew not whether
your grace had sent them to trie vs, whether we would
doe iustice, or whether it were of their owne volun-
tarie will or not, we cannot tell, and therefore for
our owne safegard we sent him to ward where he
wanteth nothing that is fit for his grace.

King Hen. 4. Stand aside vntill we haue further
deliberated on your answere.

                                            Exit Maior.

Hen. 4. Ah Harry, Harry, now thrice accursed
          Harry,
    That hath gotten a sonne which with greefe
    Will end his fathers dayes.
    Oh my sonne, a Prince thou art, I a Prince
          indeed,
    And to deserue punishment
    And well haue they done, and like faithfull sub-
          iects:
    Discharge them and let them go.

                                            Exit omnes.

.   .   .   .

A little later the Lord Chief Justice is conducting
the trial of one Cuthbert Cutter, a follower of Prince
Hal's, for having robbed 'a poore Carrier vpon Gads
hill in Kent.' The Prince enters, with 'Ned and Tom,'
and demands the release of his man who has but
robbed 'in iest.' The Chief Justice is courteous but
resolute.

    Hen. 5. Tell me, my lord, shall I haue my man?
    Iudge. I cannot, my lord.
    Hen. 5. But will you not let him go?
    Iudge. I am sorrie his case is so ill.
    Hen. 5. Tush, case me no casings, shall I haue my
          man?
    Iudge. I cannot, nor I may not, my lord.

Hen. 5. No: then I will haue him.
                    He giueth him a box on the eare.
Ned. Gogs wounds, my lord, shal I cut off his head?
Hen. 5. No, I charge you draw not your swords,
    But get you hence, prouyde a noyse of Musitians,
    Away, be gone.
                              Exeunt the Theefe.
Iudge. Well, my Lord, I am content to take it at
    your hands.
Hen. 5. Nay, and you be not you shall haue more.
Iudge. Why, I pray you, my Lord, who am I?
Hen. 5. You, who knowes not you?
    Why man, you are the Lord chiefe Justice of
    England.
Iudge. Your grace hath said truth, therefore in
striking me in this place, you greatly abuse me, and
not me onely but also your father: whose liuely person here in this place I doo represent. And therefore to teach you what prerogatiues meane, I commit
you to the Fleete, Vntill we haue spoken to your
father.
Hen. 5. Why then belike you meane to send me to
the Fleete?
Iudge. I, indeed, and therefore carry him away.
                    Exeunt Hen. 5. with the Officers.

The scene of the Prince's repentance and reconciliation with his father, which Shakespeare uses in
1 Henry IV, in *The Famous Victories* immediately
precedes the following scene in the King's death-
chamber. The King is sleeping.

    Enter Lord of Exeter and Oxford.

Exe. Come easily, my Lord, for waking of the
        King.
Hen. 4. Now, my Lords.
Oxf. How doth your Grace feele yourselfe?
Hen. 4. Somewhat better after my sleepe,

But good my lords take off my crowne,
Remove my chair a little backe, and set me right.
Ambo. And please your grace, the crowne is taken
    away.
Hen. 4. The Crowne taken away,
    Good my lord of Oxford, go see who hath done
        this deed:
    No doubt tis some vilde traitor that hath done it,
    To depriue my sonne.   They that would do it
        now
    Would seeke to scrape and scrawle for it after
        my death.

Enter Lord of Oxford with the Prince.

Oxf. Here and please your Grace,
Is my Lord the yong Prince with the Crowne.
Hen. 4. Why how now my sonne?
    I had thought the last time I had you in school-
        ing,
    And do you now begin againe?
    Doest thou thinke the time so long
    That thou wouldest haue it before the
    Breath be out of my mouth?
Hen. 5. Most soueraign Lord, and welbeloued
        father,
    I came into your Chamber to comfort the melan-
        choly
    Soule of your bodie, and finding you at that
        time
    Past all recouerie, and dead to my thinking,
    God is my witness: and what should I doo
    But with weeping tears lament the death of you
        my father,
    And after that seeing the Crowne I tooke it:
    And tell me my father, who might better take
        it then I,
    After your death?   But seeing you liue

I most humbly render it into your Maiesties
 hands
And the happiest man aliue, that my father liue:
And liue my Lord and Father for euer.
Hen. 4. Stand vp my sonne,
 Thine answere hath sounded wel in mine eares,
 For I must nedes confesse that I was in a very
  sound sleepe.
 But come neare my sonne,
 And let me put thee in possession whilst I liue.
Hen. 5. Well may I take it at your maiesties hands,
 But it shall neuer touch my head so long as my
  father liues.

       He taketh the crowne.

The King blesses his son, prophesies a glorious
reign, calls for music, draws the curtains of his bed,
and dies. After the coronation of the new King
there is a conversation between the King and three of
his old followers, Ned, Tom, and Iockey, who accost
him as he appears in state with the Archbishop of
Canterbury, and remind him of his promise to make
Ned Lord Chief Justice.

Hen. 5. I prethee Ned, mend thy manners,
 And be more modester in thy tearmes,
 For my vnfeigned greefe is not to be ruled by
  thy flattering
 And dissembling talke. Thou saiest I am
  chaunged,
 So I am indeed, and so must thou be and that
  quickly,
 Or else I must cause thee to be chaunged.
Tom. I trust we haue not offended your grace no
 way.
Hen. 5. Ah, Tom, your former life greeves me,
 And makes me to abandon and abolish your
  company for euer.

And therefore not vpon paine of deeth to ap-
    proch my presence
By ten miles space. Then if I heare wel of you,
It may be I will do somewhat for you,
Otherwise looke for no more fauour at my hands
Then at any other mans. And therefore be gone,
We haue other matters to talke on.

Exeunt Knights.

APPENDIX B

The History of the Play

The success of *Henry IV, Part I,* led Shakespeare,
apparently, to write the second part as a sequel.
The date of its composition may be definitely stated
as lying somewhere between 1596 and 1599. The
death of Amurath III, to which reference is made in
V. ii. 48, occurred in 1596; and in Ben Jonson's
Every Man out of his Humour (Act V. sc. ii.), written in 1599, reference is made to Justice Silence.
That *Henry IV, Part II,* was written before *Henry V*
is evidenced by the unfulfilled promise in the Epilogue of the present play (see the note on that passage).

An acting version of the play, the only known
contemporary Quarto edition, was printed in 1600
and entered on the Stationers' Register on August
23 of that year. The full text of the play appeared
for the first time in the First Folio in 1623. Of the
many contemporary allusions to the play of *Henry
IV* and the characters of the play, the following
refer unquestionably to *Part II.*

(1) Sir Charles Percy, third son of the twentieth
Earl of Northumberland, Lord of Dumbleton in
Gloucestershire, a follower of the Earl of Essex, and

an admirer, perhaps a friend, of Shakespeare's, writes in a letter dated December 27, 1600 (?): "I am here so pestered with country business that I shall not be able as yet to come to London. If I stay here long in this fashion, at my return you will find me so dull that I shall be taken for Justice Shallow or Justice Silence."

(2) Dekker in *Satiromastix* (1602), *Ad Lectorem,* refers to Master Justice Shallow.

(3) Ben Jonson in *Epicœne* (1609), II. v., refers to Doll Tearsheet.

Of early performances and players of *Henry IV, Part II,* there are even fewer records than there are of *Part I.* James Wright in his *Historia Histrionica* (1699) says that 'before the wars' Lowin acted Falstaff 'with mighty applause.' Pepys, who attended at least three revivals of the first part of the play between 1660 and 1668, makes no mention of any Restoration revival of the second part. In 1700 Betterton, after a triumphant revival of *Part I,* undertook a revision and revival of *Part II.* His version held the stage for many years, and is reprinted in Lacy's *Acting Edition of Old Plays.* Chetwood tells an amusing anecdote concerning Betterton's interpretation of the part of Falstaff in *Part II.* Johnson, an actor, while playing in Dublin, had seen Baker, a master-pavior, play Falstaff. Upon his return to England he gave Mr. Betterton the manner of Baker's playing, which the great actor not only approved of, but imitated, and allowed that it was better than his own.

Betterton's arrangement of the play was as follows:

Act I begins with I. ii.; then follow the scene at the Archbishop's, and the arrest of Falstaff from Act II.

Act II contains the rest of Shakespeare's Act II, with the Warkworth Castle scenes omitted.

Act III begins with the scene at Shallow's house, but the rest of the act follows Shakespeare.

Act IV begins with the King's soliloquy on sleep, taken from Act III; then comes the scene of the King's death, followed by the scene in which Silence sings; and the act closes with the interview between the Lord Chief Justice and King Henry V.

In Act V, Betterton omits the comic scenes (i. and iv.), and opens the act with the King's progress *to* Westminster Abbey. Falstaff is rebuked, but is not sent to the Fleet, and the play concludes with an abridgment of the first Act of *Henry V*.

Betterton had the good taste not to tamper with Shakespeare's wording to any great extent.

On December 17, 1720, at Drury Lane, the play was revived again. It was acted five nights successively and once afterwards. It was in this revival that Cibber first appeared as Justice Shallow and made 'one of the great successes of the day.' Mills was Falstaff, and Wilks the Prince. Eleven years later (1731) came another Drury Lane revival, with Mills as the Prince, Harper as Falstaff, and Cibber still playing Shallow. Five years later (1736) the same company, with the exception of Harper, produced the play again at Drury Lane for the benefit of the great Quin, who played Falstaff. In 1744 and 1749 there were revivals at the Covent Garden Theatre, Quin again playing Falstaff.

A performance at Drury Lane in 1758 was made notable by Garrick's first appearance in the rôle of the King. He had appeared as Hotspur in *Part I* twelve years before, but had not achieved great success in that rôle. As the King in *Part II* 'his figure did not assist him, but the forcible expression of his countenance, and his energy of utterance, made ample amends for the defect of person.'

On December 11, 1761, and for twenty-two consecutive days, *King Henry IV, Part II,* was presented at Covent Garden in honor of the coronation of King George III. For this performance an elaborate coronation pageant was devised which was used again in 1821 by Macready at the time of the coronation of William IV. Other revivals occurred at Drury Lane in 1764 and 1777, and at Covent Garden in 1773, 1784, and 1804. A sensational feature of the 1773 performance was the appearance of an anonymous 'Gentleman' as the King, 'his first performance on any stage,' and of Mrs. Lessingham, for whose benefit the play was given, as Prince Hal. In the 1804 production John Philip Kemble played the King, and Charles Kemble the Prince. Charles Kemble again appeared as the Prince in Macready's production in June, July, and August, 1821.

Of Macready's performance he himself writes in his *Reminiscences;* 'Kemble had revived the play in 1804, but produced little effect. Garrick had not given the prominence he had expected to the part of the King, and for these reasons I begged to be excused from appearing in it. But my objections were set aside. . . . To every line of it I gave the most deliberate attention, and felt the full power of its pathos. The audience hung intently on every word. The admission of the perfect success of the performance was without dissent. The revival rewarded the managers with houses crowded to the ceiling for many nights, nor was this attributable to the pageant only, for the acting was of the highest order. Fawcett was the best Falstaff then upon the stage, but he more excelled in other parts.' The perfection of Macready's success was not, however, 'without dissent.' 'An old playgoer,' in a letter to Tallis's *Dramatic Magazine* for April, 1851, says of Macready's Henry IV: "In this rôle he approached nearest to an elocutionist, but generally the effect of his declamation was unpleasant, harsh, and grating. Kemble's poses were studied but graceful, not like the stiff upright *posés* of Macready wherein I have often wondered how he could preserve his equilibrium."

On March 17, 1853, in his ninth season at Sadler's Wells, Samuel Phelps produced *King Henry IV, Part II*, he himself playing the double rôle of the King and Justice Shallow. Contemporary reviews speak of his complete triumph, and say that sceptical critics are now converted to this as a stage play. Phelps used Betterton's version, and revived the play again in London in 1864 and in 1874. In the 1874 production Forbes-Robertson, aged 21, appeared as Prince Hal. William Winter records an interesting anecdote of the first rehearsal. Phelps, after watching Forbes-Robertson for a time, said: 'Young man, I see that you know nothing about this. Come to my room tonight.'

The play has been practically unknown on the American stage. There were twenty-six revivals of *Part I* in America in the eighteenth century, but apparently none of *Part II*. In the nineteenth century the American comedian, James H. Hackett, played the part of Falstaff almost annually from 1830 to 1870, in both England and America, but it was the Falstaff of *Part I* and of *The Merry Wives*. In 1895-1896 Miss Julia Marlowe played the part of Prince Hal in an abridged version of the two parts of the play; and in 1896-1897 Daly planned a revival which never got beyond rehearsal. Miss Ada Rehan was to play Prince Hal, and James Lewis, Falstaff. The Delta Psi Dramatic Club of Harvard University gave a creditable amateur performance of *Part II* in the winter of 1915-1916.

APPENDIX C

The Text of the Present Edition

The text of the present edition is, in the main, by permission of the Oxford University Press, that of the Oxford Shakespeare, edited by the late W. J. Craig. Stage directions, when not bracketed, are from either the First Quarto or the First Folio or both; bracketed stage directions are modern. The title of the play is from the First Quarto. The Dramatis Personæ are as given in the First Folio under the caption 'The Actors' Names.'

In II. ii. 131-149 the present editor has substituted the original assignment of speeches, in ll. 131, 135, as found in both Quarto and Folio, for Craig's assignment, as there seems to be no sufficient reason for emendations. He has also assigned ll. 139-148 to the Prince. Craig divides as follows:

131-133 *Poins.* Sir John . . . certificate.
134   *Prince.* Peace.
135-149 *Poins.* I will . . . eat it.

Many minor departures from the Oxford text have been made in this edition in an attempt to arrive at a consistent text. The Oxford editor has in the majority of cases followed the readings of the First Quarto, but in about fifty instances he has adopted the slightly different expressions used in the more formal and less colloquial Folio text. For example, in the scenes of low comedy, *he* in the Folio is almost invariably *a'* in the Quarto; *is it* is *is 't; it is* is *'tis;* etc. The Oxford editor has used sometimes the formal, sometimes the informal expression. He sometimes follows the Folio in correcting the grammar and the mispronunciations of Mistress Quickly and Justice Shallow, and sometimes does not; he frequently omits the oaths found in the Quarto and expurgated in the Folio, but more frequently includes them. The present editor has not thought it wise to burden his pages with a long list of the minor changes he has made in the Oxford text. His policy has been to follow, in general, the more colloquial Quarto text.

In the following list of other variants the readings of the present edition precede the colon, Craig's readings follow it, and the Quarto or Folio authority is given wherever involved:

Ind. 35	hole QF: hold
I. i. 33	comes QF: come
ii. 5	moe Q: more F
44	through QF: thorough
132	it QF: its
II. i. 2	action QF: exion
6	Sirrah!—: Sirrah, QF
82	all I have Q: all, all I have F
184	my lord Q: my good lord F
ii. 21	another Q: one other F
66	an QF: a
75	those QF: these
82	*Poins* QF: *Bard.*
123	kin QF: akin
137	he sure Q: sure he F
iii. 63	his QF: its
iv. 42	a pox damn you Q: omit F
51	Yea, joy Q: Ay, marry F
91	debuty Q: deputy F
93	Wedesday Q: Wednesday F
142	but I will Q: I will (passage omitted in F)
171	faitors (faters Q): fates F
194	fortune Q: fortuna F
298	shalt have Q: thou shalt have F
428-9	Come! (*She comes blubbered.*) Yea, will you come, Doll? Q: omit F
III. ii. 210	field QF: fields
339	invisible: invincible QF
IV. ii. 14	mischiefs QF: mischief
v. 146	inward, true, and Q: true and inward F
V. iii. 141	Blessed Q: Happy F
142	to Q: unto F

iv. 2   that I might die Q: I might die F
  11   wert Q: hadst F
v. 25   best, Q: most F

APPENDIX D

SUGGESTIONS FOR COLLATERAL READING

A. C. Bradley: *The Rejection of Falstaff* in *Oxford Lectures on Poetry*. London, 1909.

George Brandes: *William Shakespeare, a Critical Study*. London, 1880.

Stopford Brooke: *Ten More Plays of Shakespeare*. London, 1913.

Beverley E. Warner: *English History in Shakespeare's Plays*. New York, 1894.

See also the corresponding appendix to *Henry IV, Part I,* in this edition.

INDEX OF WORDS GLOSSED

(Figures in full-faced type refer to page-numbers)